Heroes and Villains

Pol Pot

Andy Koopmans

LUCENT BOOKS
An imprint of Thomson Gale, a part of The Thomson Corporation

Detroit • New York • San Francisco • San Diego • New Haven, Conn. • Waterville, Maine • London • Munich

To the people of Cambodia

For more information, contact
Lucent Books
27500 Drake Rd.
Farmington Hills, MI 48331-3535
Or you can visit our Internet site at http://www.gale.com

LIBRARY OF CONGRESS CATALOGING-IN-PUBLICATION DATA

Koopmans, Andy.
  Pol Pot / by Andy Koopmans.
    p. cm. — (Heroes and villains series)
  Includes bibliographical references and index.
  ISBN 1-59018-596-X (hardcover : alk. paper)
  1. Pol Pot—Juvenile literature. 2. Cambodia—History—20th century—Juvenile literature. 3. Heads of state—Cambodia—Biography—Juvenile literature.
I. Title. II. Series.
  DS554.83.P65K66 2005
  959.604'2'092—dc22
                                                    2004016754

Printed in the United States of America

Contents

FOREWORD   4

INTRODUCTION
Tyrant or True Believer?   6

CHAPTER 1
A Privileged Youth   9

CHAPTER 2
A Political Awakening   20

CHAPTER 3
Revolutionary   32

CHAPTER 4
Rising to Power   45

CHAPTER 5
Ruler in the Shadows   56

CHAPTER 6
Brother Number One   71

CHAPTER 7
Leader in Exile   81

Notes   95
Chronology   98
For Further Reading   101
Works Consulted   103
Index   106
Picture Credits   111
About the Author   112

Foreword

Good and evil are an ever-present feature of human history. Their presence is reflected through the ages in tales of great heroism and extraordinary villainy. Such tales provide insight into human nature, whether they involve two people or two thousand, for the essence of heroism and villainy is found in deeds rather than in numbers. It is the deeds that pique our interest and lead us to wonder what prompts a man or woman to perform such acts.

Samuel Johnson, the eminent eighteenth-century English writer, once wrote, "The two great movers of the human mind are the desire for good, and fear of evil." The pairing of desire and fear, possibly two of the strongest human emotions, helps explain the intense fascination people have with all things good and evil—and, by extension, heroic and villainous.

People are attracted to the person who reaches into a raging river to pull a child from what could have been a watery grave for both, and to the person who risks his or her own life to shepherd hundreds of desperate black slaves to safety on the Underground Railroad. We wonder what qualities these heroes possess that enable them to act against self-interest, and even their own survival. We also wonder if, under similar circumstances, we would behave as they do.

Evil, on the other hand, horrifies as well as intrigues us. Few people can look upon the drifter who mutilates and kills a neighbor or the dictator who presides over the torture and murder of thousands of his own citizens without feeling a sense of revulsion. And yet, as Joseph Conrad writes, we experience "the fascination of the abomination." How else to explain the overwhelming success of a book such as Truman Capote's *In Cold Blood*, which examines in horrifying detail a vicious and senseless murder that took place in the American heartland in the 1960s? The popularity of murder mysteries and Court TV are also evidence of the human fascination with villainy.

Most people recoil in the face of such evil. Yet most feel a deep-seated curiosity about the kind of person who could commit a terrible act. It is perhaps a reflection of our innermost fears that we wonder whether we could resist or stand up to such behavior in our presence or even if we ourselves possess the capacity to commit such terrible crimes.

The Lucent Books Heroes and Villains series capitalizes on our fascination with the perpetrators of both good and evil by introducing readers to some of history's most revered heroes and hated villains. These include heroes such as Frederick Douglass, who knew firsthand the humiliation of slavery and, at great risk to himself, publicly fought to abolish the institution of slavery in America. It also includes villains such as Adolf Hitler, who is remembered both for the devastation of Europe and for the murder of 6 million Jews and thousands of Gypsies, Slavs, and others whom Hitler deemed unworthy of life.

Each book in the Heroes and Villains series examines the life story of a hero or villain from history. Generous use of primary and secondary source quotations gives readers eyewitness views of the life and times of each individual as well as enlivens the narrative. Notes and annotated bibliographies provide stepping-stones to further research.

TYRANT OR TRUE BELIEVER?

As secretary general of the Communist Party of Kampuchea (CPK) and the prime minister of the revolutionary government of Democratic Kampuchea (DK), Pol Pot was at the top of a group of leaders whose policies and actions led to the deaths of 1.5 million to 3 million Cambodians in the years 1975–1979. Beyond the scope of those deaths, millions of others—the maimed, the homeless, the orphaned, the widowed—suffered during those years, and many more thousands of people died or were harmed in the years to follow for reasons directly or indirectly related to the Pol Pot regime.

Many historians have emphasized that leaders from other countries—particularly France, the United States, China, and Vietnam—as well as King Norodom Sihanouk, the monarch of Cambodia, and his followers, share a portion of the blame for the tragedies Cambodia experienced under the Pol Pot regime. However, just as Adolf Hitler was the predominant villain of the Nazi Holocaust, Pol Pot was the predominant villain of the Cambodian genocide and the main architect of his brutal regime.

Unlike Hitler or many other infamous leaders such as Mao Tse-tung or Joseph Stalin, relatively few personal details are known about Pol Pot. This is due in part to Pol Pot's purposeful attempt to hide—even erase—his prerevolutionary identity of Saloth Sar. In doing so, he also invented a fictitious past for himself that hid his privileged background and made it more compatible with his revolutionary rhetoric. Further, Pol Pot did not often write or speak about himself, and when he did, he often did not tell the truth. He also avoided the spotlight for most of his reign, preferring to hide behind the anonymity of the CPK.

However, biographers have pieced together what is known about Pol Pot and meshed it with historical and political events and people surrounding him to create a portrait of the Communist ruler. The picture is incomplete, leaving many questions unanswered, and at times the facts seem contradictory. For one example, those who knew Saloth Sar/Pol Pot personally often had difficulty reconciling his affable and charming personality with the horrific crimes of his regime. For another, little is known about what motivated Pol Pot to take one of the most important steps of his life: choosing to become a Communist. Most important, such holes leave begging fundamental questions: Was

Known to the world as Pol Pot, Saloth Sar headed a regime in Cambodia whose policies caused the deaths of 1.5 to 3 million people from 1975 to 1979.

Pictured in this museum exhibit are just a small number of the inmates who perished in one of Pol Pot's numerous prison camps.

Pol Pot a purposefully wanton tyrant bent on destroying his people or a misguided, horribly inept, deranged true believer? Did he refuse or fail to see the mistakes he made or the pain he caused, or did he perhaps believe they were worth the price for the achievement of what he considered a utopian society?

What is known about Pol Pot is that, like many of his generation, and like many colonized or oppressed people all over the world following World War II, he wanted to achieve independence for his country. He wanted to lead a Communist revolution to rid Cambodia of the colonial French and the series of governments that succeeded them, all of which Pol Pot saw as corrupt, unfair, and tyrannical. Unfortunately, his own government proved to be even worse than the others, particularly for the very people the Communist revolution had ostensibly been fought to help, the common Cambodians.

Chapter One

A Privileged Youth

Pol Pot, born Saloth Sar, was born into a peasant family in Cambodia. However, because of his family's connections with the royal palace, Saloth was able to pursue an education typically reserved for a small minority of privileged and wealthy people in the French-ruled country. The limited number of schools in Cambodia and the distance of these schools from his home made it necessary for Saloth to leave his family at an early age to attend boarding school. Thus he traded a traditional family-oriented life for one of solitude and opportunity.

Among the opportunities education afforded him were becoming fluent in French and making acquaintances with children of prominent and powerful families. These opportunities not only prepared him for higher education but also, perhaps more important, allowed him to make political connections that would help steer the course of his life. Saloth was at best a lazy and mediocre student, yet despite his lack of academic strength, by the age of twenty-one he had already made political connections that gained him a prestigious scholarship to study abroad.

An Ancient Heritage

Saloth Sar was born on May 19, 1928, in the village of Prek Sbauv in the province of Kompong Thom, Cambodia. He was the seventh son and the eighth of nine children born to Saloth Pen, a farmer, and his wife, Sok Nem, respected as a pious and good woman by her community. The family owned twenty-two acres of rice paddy, seven acres of garden land, and six buffalo, making it a prosperous household able to produce enough rice to feed twenty people daily.

Like most people living in Cambodia at the time, Saloth and his parents were ethnic Khmer, descendants of the earliest known indigenous people of the region who had probably inhabited Cambodia since before 4200 B.C. During Saloth's childhood, the daily life of Khmer people was very similar to what it had been for many centuries. As historian Ben Kiernan writes, "Rich or poor everyone tilled the fields, fished the river, cooked tasty soups, raised children, propitiated the local spirits . . . or thronged Buddhist festivities in Kompong Thom's pagoda."[1] Like their ancestors, they also spoke the Khmer language, which dated back to the early Christian era, and honored the kings of Cambodia, who were thought by most Cambodian peasants to be gods or demigods.

From approximately the ninth to the fourteenth century, Cambodia was the center of the Khmer Empire, which at its height in the twelfth and thirteenth centuries had encompassed much of present-day Southeast Asia. Many of the structures built by the kings of the Khmer Empire still exist at ancient Angkor, the imperial capital, located in what is now northwestern Cambodia. The remains of the structures, particularly the walled city of Angkor Thom and the temple complex of Angkor Wat, are testament to the far-reaching power and great wealth of the empire at its height.

In the centuries that followed the waning of the Khmer Empire, Cambodia shrank because of enemy invasions from Vietnam and Thailand. Eventually, the empire and the names of kings were forgotten by the Khmer people. In 1863, at the request of the monarch, Prince Norodom, the weakened kingdom came under the control of the French, who had also taken control of neighboring Vietnam in the 1850s.

Life Under French Rule

When Saloth was born, Cambodia had been a French protectorate for sixty-five years. As such, Cambodia was not

An Isolated, Homogeneous Culture

As Ben Kiernan writes in his book The Pol Pot Regime: Race, Power, and Genocide in Cambodia Under the Khmer Rouge, 1975–79, *in contrast to other Indochinese nations, the Cambodia into which Saloth Sar was born was predominately a rural and ethnically and religiously homogeneous culture, long cut off by the French colonial government from foreign influences.*

Pre-Revolutionary Cambodia was 80 percent peasant, 80 percent Khmer, and 80 percent Buddhist. First, it was an overwhelmingly rural economy. Its village society was decentralized, its economy unintegrated, dominated by subsistence rice cultivation. Compared to Vietnam's, its villagers participated much less in village-oriented activities. They were often described as individualistic; the nuclear family was the social core . . . [and] most villagers usually did not recall their grandparents' names. Subsistence was usually a personal or family matter. . . .

Second, Cambodia was ethnically quite homogenous, as were Thailand and Vietnam. But unlike its neighbors, Cambodia had much less exposure to cultural influence, which, when it came, was potentially destabilizing. Mostly as a result of French colonial policy in Indochina, Cambodia acquired a substantial but unintegrated minority population. . . . Eighty percent of Cambodia's residents were Khmer, but Chinese and Vietnamese dominated the cities. . . .

Third, Cambodia was overwhelmingly Buddhist. The Khmer, Lao, and Thai are all Theravada Buddhist, while Chinese and Vietnamese are usually Mahayana Buddhist. . . . Cambodia's non-Buddhist communities are limited to Catholic Vietnamese, Islamic Cham, and animist highland tribes.

officially possessed by France and was still supposedly ruled internally by the monarch, King Monivong, and protected by France on a national level. However, in reality, the French directed the governing of the country through the king and treated Cambodia as a colony under their tight control. The French saw the Cambodian people as childlike and largely incapable of ruling themselves.

Under French rule, the landscape of Cambodia changed in many ways, particularly in the first decades of the twentieth century. Roads were built throughout the kingdom, and a railroad was constructed between the country's two largest cities, Phnom Penh, the capital, and Battambang. The advances allowed the French to better exploit the rural rice economy, which, along with newly constructed rubber plantations, created an economic boom during the 1920s. The taxes collected on the exports were in part channeled into public-works projects to beautify the capital and to provide electricity to the smaller towns.

Except for the Cambodian elite, however, life under French rule was largely unchanged and predominantly limited to peasant farming. Even in the cities, the economy was dominated by the growing immigrant Chinese business class and Vietnamese workers, who were given preference over the indigenous people.

Moving to Phnom Penh

Further, the French provided few opportunities for the Cambodian peasantry to gain an education. Under the French, Cambodian intellectual institutions had declined. Until 1936, there was no opportunity for secondary education, and primary schooling was the responsibility of the Buddhist monks at *wat* (temple) schools. Only a handful of children got the opportunity for even this limited education.

Saloth was fortunate that his family was connected to the royal palace in Phnom Penh through a cousin, Luk Khun Meak. She had been a member of the royal ballet at the palace and had become one of King Monivong's wives. She even bore him a child. In 1925 she had brought Saloth's older brother Loth Suong to Phnom Penh, where he had become a clerk at the palace and married a member of the royal ballet, Chea Samy.

In 1934, when Saloth was six, his parents sent him to live with the family in Loth Suong's large house on Trasak Paem Street in the capital. He enrolled at Botumbodey, a monastery near the royal palace. Loth Suong was a strict guardian. One neighbor girl said that he "was very serious and would not gamble or allow children such as myself to play near his home."[2] For his part, Saloth gave his new guardian little trouble and was an obedient student at school. Loth Suong said he was "a lovely child" and Chea Samy said that he "had no difficulties with other students, no fights or quarrels."[3]

After Saloth left the monastery in 1936 when he was eight years old, his cousin Meak paid his tuition to attend a

King Monivong (left) marches at the head of his entourage during his 1935 coronation ceremony. Ruling as a puppet of the French government, the king wielded no true power.

private French Catholic school, École Miche, near the palace. He spent six years there, learning about Christianity and becoming fluent in French. Again, classmates remembered him as a "very charming"[4] child.

High School

By the time Saloth had graduated from primary school in 1942, a new generation of Cambodian elites, educated at the country's one high school, Lycée Sisowath in Phnom Penh, or in prestigious schools in Saigon, Vietnam, had influenced government policy enough to encourage the creation of more secondary schools. Most

of the Cambodian elite who were able to afford secondary school went to Lycée Sisowath. Saloth was one of twenty boys selected to be the first class at a new high school, Collège Norodom Sihanouk, named after the new ruler, King Sihanouk, who had been crowned in 1941 following the death of King Monivong. After Monivong's death the French had selected his nineteen-year-old nephew, a temperamental playboy named Norodom Sihanouk, to succeed him. The new school named in his honor was located in Kompong Cham, the country's third largest city and a bustling center of commerce to the northeast of Phnom Penh.

Saloth again left his family behind to pursue his education. He and his nineteen classmates lived together in dormitories on campus and became close companions. Among his fellow students were several boys who, like Saloth, later became Communists. Two of these boys, Hu Nim and Khieu Samphan, both a few years younger than Saloth, later became his close associates and members of the Pol Pot regime. Saloth's closest companion at Collège Sihanouk was Lon Non, brother to Lon Nol, who later became one of Pol Pot's most formidable political enemies.

The students studied literature, geography, science, and philosophy. They also played sports and studied musical instruments. Saloth took up the violin as well as basketball and soccer. One classmate commented on his sports skills: "He was a pretty good [sports] player, but not outstanding."[5] Saloth was reportedly an affable but mediocre student who preferred talking and playing with friends to studying. One classmate said, "His manner was straight-forward, pleasant, and very polite."[6]

Classes at the French-administered school were conducted in French, and students were discouraged by the mostly French faculty from speaking their native Khmer language, even among themselves. However, one teacher, a Khmer named Khvan Siphan, was different. Khvan was honest, helpful, and affectionate toward the students and served as an inspiration to many of them, including Saloth.

A brother of Pol Pot's high school friend Lon Non, Lon Nol became one of the dictator's most formidable political enemies.

Stirrings of Nationalism

Although there is no indication that Saloth or his fellow students were politically engaged while in high school, they were certainly aware of the dynamic political changes that occurred during their time at Collège Sihanouk. Whether or not they knew it at the time, many of these changes had a direct impact on Saloth and his fellow future Communists in particular.

The changes in the country, influenced by various world events, centered on the rising nationalist sentiment and activism in favor of Cambodian independence from France. During the 1930s, nationalism had begun to grow among the people and Cambodian government officials. Although the sentiment was slow to spread, the arrival and aftermath of World War II set in motion a chain of events that would result in cries for independence in colonies all over the world, including the area of Southeast Asia known as Indochina, encompassing the French colonies of Vietnam and Cambodia (and Laos, which would be recognized as a separate state under French control in 1949).

In 1940 Germany invaded and occupied France. Then, acting through the occupied French government, the Germans allowed their Japanese allies to send troops into northwestern Cambodia in 1941. The Japanese, who already occupied China, wished to extend their range of influence south through Indochina. By 1945 there were six to nine thousand Japanese troops in Cambodia.

On July 20, 1942, around the time Saloth began school in Kompong Cham, a group of five hundred Buddhist monks and two hundred civilian Cambodians, inspired by the Japanese expansion, led a march through the streets of Phnom Penh to the residence of the French colonial officials. They marched to protest the brutality of French occupying forces and their presence in Cambodia generally. It was a

Cambodian students study in Phnom Penh. Saloth himself studied at Collège Sihanouk, a new high school in the city of Kompong Cham.

bold maneuver that had historic consequences. The leaders of the march, nation-
alists Son Ngoc Thanh and Pach Chhoeun,
believed that the Japanese would support
them. However, they were mistaken, and
the French arrested many protesters, including Pach Chhoeun. Son Ngoc Thanh fled
to Japan, but not before becoming a national hero.

A Brief Independence

After the Germans surrendered in 1945,
the new French government under General
Charles de Gaulle joined with the United
States and Great Britain to fight the
Japanese. In March 1945, still occupying
Cambodia, the Japanese decided to make
their move. Executing a *coup de force*, the
Japanese invaded Cambodia, Laos, and
Vietnam, arresting and imprisoning French
officials, military personnel, and civilians.
Among these were Saloth's French teachers at Collège Sihanouk, who were replaced
by less experienced Khmer teachers. The
Japanese government then encouraged the
French colonies to declare their independence, which all of them did. On March
11, 1945, Sihanouk announced a newly
formed state, the independent Kingdom
of Cambodia. Son Ngoc Thanh returned
in May to a parade of more than ten thousand people. In August, he became prime
minister.

Independence, however, was short-
lived. On August 6 and 9, the United
States dropped two atomic bombs on Japan
at Hiroshima and Nagasaki, respectively.
The Japanese surrendered within a few

days. In September British troops arrived
in Cambodia to arrest the Japanese and free
the French prisoners. Other French officials began returning, and by October 1945
the Kingdom of Cambodia had come to
the end of its short independence. Son
Ngoc Thanh was tried for treason and
exiled to France.

First Political Action

Along with most Cambodians, Saloth was
disappointed with the undoing of Cambodian independence. However, when the
French returned to take back power, they
discovered that reasserting control over their
former colonies was not easy. For Cambodia, the short taste of independence had
been very appealing, and the French were
forced to make some concessions in power.
In 1946, they issued a declaration that
granted Cambodia the right to a constitution and the formation of political parties.

Immediately political parties were
formed for the election of a congress to
write the country's first constitution. The
strongest of the parties was the Democratic Party, which was popular with
monks, teachers, civil servants, and the
country's newly educated young people,
including Saloth. The Democrats became
a powerful political force, opposed by the
French and Sihanouk, both of whom were
afraid the party could win the upcoming
National Assembly elections. This made
the Democrats a threat that could take
away their power and give it to the people.

When National Assembly elections
were held the following year, Saloth report-

The Japanese formally surrender to the Allies in 1945. During World War II, the Japanese invaded and occupied Cambodia.

edly worked for the Democratic campaign. Although it is not known exactly when Saloth left Collège Sihanouk, he returned to Phnom Penh without receiving a baccalaureate (equivalent to a high school degree).

The party won two-thirds of the seats in the National Assembly, but in an effort to undermine the victory, Sihanouk had seventeen Democratic members of the assembly arrested on fabricated criminal charges. They were taken out of the country to Saigon, where some of them were tortured before being released without ever being charged. Then, in September 1949, Sihanouk took advantage of a provision in the constitution that allowed him to dissolve the assembly and rule by decree, meaning he could make and enact laws without approval of elected representatives. He also illegally postponed the required elections for a new National Assembly until September 1951.

Technical School

While the Democrats fought with Sihanouk and the French for power through legal means, guerrilla resistance groups sprang up in the countryside. Some were assisted by Vietnamese Vietminh in Cambodia. Since 1946 the Vietminh had been fighting a successful resistance to French reassertion of power in Vietnam. They hoped to enlist Cambodians in their movement in exchange for helping the Cambodians struggle against the French.

Despite the direct-action appeal of the guerrilla movements, most Cambodians, including Saloth, supported the Democrats and legal means to achieve Cambodian independence. At this point, Saloth was not a political activist but a student looking forward to a practical career.

Phnom Penh

In Brother Number One: A Political Biography of Pol Pot, *David P. Chandler describes Phnom Penh as it was in the early 1930s when Saloth Sar was growing up.*

When Sar was growing up in the 1930s, Phnom Penh was a sleepy, sun-drenched town that had been established as the capital of a French Protectorate in 1866. . . . The city had the form of a rectangle, running north and south along the eastern bank of the Tonle Sap River, which flowed in to the much larger Mekong River at that point. Many public buildings, like the post office, the library, and the railroad station, were reminiscent of their counterparts in southern France. So were the tree-lined avenues radiating from the public gardens to the north and the shaded promenades along the river. In 1936, roughly half of its 100,000 population were immigrant Chinese and Vietnamese, who dominated the commercial sector. Its 45,000 Cambodians lived around the palace, as monks in the monasteries or bureaucrats, farmers, artisans, and petty traders in the southern and western sectors of the city. There, the Cambodians' bamboo and wooden houses—raised on stilts and surrounded by mango and banana trees, with domestic animals roaming underneath—were indistinguishable from rural dwellings. . . .

The center of Phnom Penh contained a bustling commercial quarter of Chinese shops, warehouses, eating stalls, and markets. To the west, parallel to the river, ran shaded trees and boulevards lined with stucco-covered villas of French civil servants, Chinese businessmen, and the French-educated Cambodian elite. At the northern edge of the city, the small hill (*phnom*) that gave the city its name was crowned by a seventeenth-century monastery and several Buddhist reliquaries.

Because Saloth's test scores were not high enough for him to graduate from Collège Sihanouk, he enrolled at École Technique, a technical school in a northern suburb of Phnom Penh. He lived on campus and studied carpentry. Little is known about his time at technical school other than that he made one of the most important friendships of his life with a young, politically active student at Lycée Sisowath named Ieng Sary, who would be a close associate and friend for fifty years.

In 1948 it seemed as though Saloth was on the path to becoming a tradesman. However, that year he received news that he had been awarded a scholarship to study radio technology in Paris. The Democrat-administered Ministry of Education had established scholarships to send Khmer students to Paris, where they were to study in fields that were at the time dominated by the minority Vietnamese population. In the previous two years, only one hundred students, most from prominent families, had been awarded the honor. Although Saloth had been a mediocre student, the Democrats apparently awarded him the scholarship in repayment for his service in the 1947 campaign.

Saloth accepted the scholarship. The honor and the thrill of studying abroad likely appealed greatly to him. However, he could not have known at the time how his years in Paris would so dramatically change the direction of his life.

Chapter Two

A POLITICAL AWAKENING

In 1949 Saloth Sar left Cambodia to study abroad on scholarship in Paris. There, in the politically charged atmosphere during the postwar years, he and several of his fellow Khmer students explored various political avenues and ideas with a mind toward their country's struggle for independence from the French. When Saloth returned to Cambodia in January, 1953, he was a member of the French Communist Party (FCP) and an eager recruit for the Vietnamese-based Indochina Communist Party (ICP).

A Great Adventure

In August 1949 Saloth left Phnom Penh for Saigon, where he and his fellow Cambodian scholarship students gathered to board the SS *Jamaique* for Marseilles, France. The twenty-one young students spent a month in the city while their passports and tickets were arranged. For the students, all in their early twenties, it was the beginning of an exciting adventure. Most of them had never seen more than their region of Cambodia, and almost none of them, Saloth included, had ever been outside the country.

Among Saloth's fellow scholarship recipients were young men who, like himself, would later rise to prominence in the Cambodian Communist Party, including Mey Mann, Chau Seng, Mey Phat, and Uch Ven. Mey Mann befriended Saloth during their time in Saigon and on board the ship and later recalled Saloth's warm personality:

[A] group of us, all with scholarships, all spent a month in Saigon waiting for our passports and getting our boat tickets. During this time I started to get to know Saloth Sar. And then we traveled together for the month-long voyage to Marseilles on a boat called the *Jamaique*. I found him amusing, sociable and courteous. . . . He was very amenable and fun . . . warm and charming and liked to joke.[7]

Student Life

The *Jamaique* crossed the Red Sea and the Mediterranean, arriving in Marseilles on

the southeast coast of France in September 1949. From there, the Khmer students dispersed. Saloth, like many of his compatriots, took the train north to Paris, where he enrolled at the Cité Universitaire de Paris. Built on an eighty-four-acre wooded park in southeastern Paris, the Cité had been built during the 1920s to encourage international students to study and exchange cultural ideas among themselves and with the French. Saloth took a room at the Indochinese pavilion near the campus,

In 1949 Saloth Sar went to Saigon, Vietnam (pictured), from which he left for France. As a student in Paris, he became fascinated with Communist ideology.

where he likely became acquainted with many of the other Khmer students attending the university. Unlike some of his fellow classmates, Saloth apparently made little effort to mix with French or other foreign students, keeping his circle of acquaintances among the other Khmer. As biographer David Chandler suggests:

> He was not at home in France. In the cold, crowded streets and cramped student quarters, he often must have felt lonely and disoriented. Although he spoke and read French fluently, he had no connections with the country . . . [and] made little effort to assimilate. . . . Perhaps in this exile, he became more consciously Cambodian than he had been at home. [8]

It is clear from accounts of people who knew him during this time that he paid little attention to his schoolwork; however, during his first year he claims to have worked hard at his studies. He reportedly was a voracious reader, and with his fluency in French was able to study French literature in its original language, including the works of Victor Hugo, Paul Verlaine, Arthur Rimbaud, and Alfred-Victor de Vigny.

During summer break in 1950, Saloth volunteered for a labor crew working in Yugoslavia, which had been a Soviet satellite state until it broke away from the USSR in 1949. There he performed manual labor amid the country's massive industrial expansion efforts. According to Saloth's

family, he had left his family's farm before he worked a day in the rice fields, so this was likely the first such experience of his life. Like his other compatriots, Saloth was likely impressed by Yugoslavia's united national efforts in building factories, energy systems, railways, and roads.

Important Acquaintances

During his years in Paris, Saloth remained in intermittent contact with his brother Loth Suong, from whom he borrowed money at times. At one point, he asked his brother to send biographical information about King Sihanouk. Loth Suong advised Saloth to stay out of politics. However, this was advice that Saloth would not follow.

In 1951 Ieng Sary and another politically radical friend, Rath Sameourn, arrived in Paris from Cambodia. Like Saloth, they had been awarded their scholarships for political activity rather than academic merit. Soon after the National Assembly was dissolved in 1948, Ieng and Rath, both students at Lycée Sisowath, had organized a student protest of the dissolution. In Paris Ieng introduced Saloth to Rath and several other Khmer who were to become crucial to Saloth's political and personal life.

Ieng introduced Saloth to two older, politically active students already in Paris: Thiounn Mumm and Keng Vannsak. Mumm was a Vietnamese-educated child of one of the most important nonroyal families in Phnom Penh. Already a member of the French Communist Party, he

A Politicized Youth

Saloth Sar and his fellow Khmer Student Association radicals were part of a newly educated generation. As Marie Alexandrine Martin writes in her book Cambodia: A Shattered Society, *these young, politicized intellectuals became vital to the upheaval in Cambodia following World War II.*

It was in Paris that the future Khmer Rouge leaders gained the attention of foreigners and created a structure that rallied the majority of the left-wing Cambodian intellectuals whose support would prove decisive in their victory.

Dissent could come only from the city and from intellectuals with rural backgrounds. For reasons that were both historical and sociological, peasants remained passive, loyal to the divine royalty or to the one who represented it, regardless of his behavior.

Nationalist ideas germinated in the heads of studious youth.... [T]he first demonstrations against the French ... came from Lycée Sisowath students and then, early in the 1940s, from lay and religious elements. At the same time that the lay group created the Democratic party, their younger comrades from the lycées of Phnom Penh, Saigon, and Hanoi experienced democracy in France. Most held scholarships from the Khmer government, and they reacted differently to the political environment: some remained outside any form of agitation while others became militants, among them the future Khmer Rouge leaders.

had been one of the first Khmer students sent on scholarship to Paris by the Democratic National Assembly. Like Saloth, Keng was also from a Cambodian family with connections to the palace. He had attended Lycée Sisowath with Ieng and had been active in the Democratic movement.

Keng arranged for Saloth to have an apartment not far from the Montparnasse district, the intellectual and artistic center of Paris during the early twentieth century. Famed artists such as Pablo Picasso, writers such as Ernest Hemingway and F.

Scott Fitzgerald, and political exiles such as Vladimir Lenin and Leon Trotsky had all spent time in the sidewalk cafés of Montparnasse during the height of the bohemian 1920s. In the late 1940s and early 1950s, the cafés were still as lively and filled with students, intellectuals, and artists discussing politics, art, and other topics.

Ieng also introduced Saloth to his fiancée, Khieu Thirith, the daughter of a prominent Cambodian judge. She and Ieng had become engaged in Phnom Penh before leaving for Paris, where

In the sidewalk cafés of Montparnasse, Saloth engaged in lively discussions about politics and art with other students.

they were to be married in the summer of 1951. She was accompanied by her older sister, Khieu Ponnary, eight years older than Saloth and already a distinguished teacher in Cambodia. Khieu Ponnary was the first woman in Cambodia to receive her baccalaureate; Khieu Thirith had followed her example and had come to Paris to study literature. Khieu Ponnary would later become Saloth's first wife, but it is not known whether their romantic involvement began in Paris or later, after their return to Cambodia in 1952.

Politicization

Like most of the hundred or so Khmer students at the Cité Universitaire, Saloth, Ieng, Rath, Mumm, and others joined the Khmer Student Association (KSA), a nonsectarian friendship organization. Cliques formed within this group, many of them along political affiliations and interests. Under the leadership of Keng and Mumm, Saloth and others associated with Ieng formed a radical leftist clique that shared an animosity toward the monarchy of King Sihanouk and French imperialism in Cambodia. Among other members of this clique were Saloth's fellow classmate from Collège Norodom Sihanouk, Khieu Samphan; Hou Yuon, a peasant-born Khmer; and several of Saloth's acquaintances from his journey to Paris, including Mey Mann.

Despite his family's ties to the palace, Saloth was probably influenced to oppose the monarchy by recent political events back home, particularly Sihanouk's disso- lution of the National Assembly in 1949. This event was followed by the signing of an agreement by the Cambodian govern- ment and the French that ostensibly made Cambodia an independent nation within the French Union. However, many thought the agreement was insufficient because it allowed the French to remain in control of economic matters and military defense and because Cambodia still had to obey

Paris

In Brother Number One: A Political Biography of Pol Pot, *David P. Chandler describes Paris during the 1940s and 1950s as home to a lively intellectual landscape in which Saloth Sar and his fellow KSA students were encouraged to explore new, radical political ideas. For Saloth it was the birthplace of a lifelong pursuit of Communist ideologies.*

The "City of Light" had retained a reputation for over a century as a vibrant intellec- tual center. In 1949, artists, politicians, writers, philosophers, and musicians mingled in the contending schools of existentialism, Postimpressionism, phenomenology, Gaullism, and communism, to name only five. New developments in these fields and many oth- ers made Paris an intoxicating place for young people engaged in tertiary study, as did the traditions of liberty and revolutionary thought. Political parties, and the newspapers affiliated with them, flourished across the ideological spectrum, giving rise to lively, acri- monious debate. For students of Saloth Sar's generation, the early 1950s were filled with passionate arguments about politics, art, and philosophy, with close friendships and late hours, with a sense of belonging to a world that was opening up in the aftermath of World War II. To understand Saloth Sar's conversion to communism, we must place him among the soot-blackened buildings, leaf-strewn avenues, and smoke-filled cafés of the Latin Quarter among thousands of young men and women who were making similar decisions. By 1951, if not before, he was caught up in a wave of optimism about the potentialities of the Communist movement. Unlike many of his contemporaries, Saloth Sar never abandoned communism or regretted his decision. Instead, he made a life-long commitment to the cause.

French dictates. Many Cambodian students and intellectuals, including Saloth, were dissatisfied and angry with Sihanouk over these matters.

The group gathered regularly at Keng Vannsak's apartment to discuss politics. Many, like Keng, were sympathetic to the Democrats; many were also admirers of Son Ngoc Thanh and the nationalist guerrilla movement. However, the group eventually gravitated toward communism for its anticolonial stance.

The students' interest in communism was no doubt influenced by the strong Communist Party in France, which had grown quite large in the postwar years. Additionally, they were likely influenced by world events of the period. During the postwar years, Communist parties had arisen in many nations around the world, particularly those that had been hard hit by the war, where poverty was rampant and unemployment was high. The late 1940s and early 1950s were also a time when support for communism was fueled by the successful Communist revolution in China in 1949 and the military confrontation between Communist and anti-Communist forces in Korea.

Mey Mann said that Saloth and many of the others in the group were gradually drawn in by Mumm and the French Communists:

Little by little the French Communist Party took us under their wing and little by little we were introduced to

Marxist doctrine. It seemed like justice, it was similar to Buddhism. It was then we decided to sacrifice ourselves to the cause, at the expense of our studies, I'm afraid.[9]

At the meetings at Keng's apartment, the group studied various Communist texts, likely including the writings of Karl Marx, Mao Tse-tung, and Joseph Stalin. Even though Communist activity was considered subversive, the French police, who were apparently aware of these meetings, were unable to break them up or arrest the students because they were not breaking the law.

Reports of Saloth's behavior at the meetings vary widely. Mey Mann recalled him as quiet and reserved: "[H]e never actively participated. . . . I didn't see anything special about him. Nothing that would make you think he would one day lead the country. He was really very ordinary."[10]

Conversely, another attendee reported that when contradicted on a point of Communist dogma, Saloth lashed out, revealing his ambitions toward power and a strict adherence to Communist Party doctrine: "It is I who will direct the revolutionary organization! I will become the secretary general [of the party]! . . . I will control the ministries, and I will see that there is no deviation from the line fixed by the central committee in the interest of the people."[11] However, this one reported outburst, whether true or not, was an anomaly; Saloth otherwise kept whatev-

中國人民解放軍華北野戰軍
政治部宣傳隊

毛主席

華北平解

Communist soldiers march through the streets of Beijing, China, in 1949. The Communist revolution in China inspired similar revolutions in Vietnam and Cambodia.

er political ambitions he had at the time to himself.

Vietnamese Influence

Among the few foreign students with whom Saloth interacted were some Vietnamese Communists. Although there was a historic animosity between the Cambodians and the Vietnamese because of centuries of territorial conflicts and invasions as well as France's preferential treatment of the Vietnamese minority in Cambodia, these students were welcomed by and had an influence on Saloth and his fellow radicals.

The Vietnamese Communists and the Khmer radicals had common enemies: France and its ally the "imperialist" United States, which was heavily financing France's war against the Vietnamese. As biographer Ben Kiernan writes:

> The longer France tried to hang onto its colony [Vietnam], and the more backing Paris got from the USA, the more Cambodians embraced an alliance based on mutual interests with their Vietnamese neighbors, disregarding historical animosities.[12]

Ho Chi Minh founded the Indochinese Communist Party in 1930 to resist the French occupation of Vietnam.

While the Khmer students dreamed of a revolution in their own country, the Vietnamese Communists were already participating in one against the French. They were members of the Indochina Communist Party, which had been created by Vietnamese Communist leader Ho Chi Minh in 1930 in resistance to the French occupation of Vietnam. By 1951, the Vietminh were waging a desperate battle and taking heavy losses. By the end of the year, over ninety thousand Vietnamese casualties had been reported.

In September 1951, needing to raise Communist armies from neighboring Laos and Cambodia to help fight the French, the ICP splintered into three parties: the Vietnam Workers Party (VWP), the Khmer People's Party (KPP)—also known as the Khmer People's Revolutionary Party (KPRP)—and the Laotian People's Party (LPP). The VWP (which was still referred to by many as the ICP) would remain senior to the other two parties, directing and supporting them as long as they did nothing to endanger or oppose the Vietnam revolution, which the VWP saw as the key event for the future of Indochinese politics. The KPP and LPP were to recruit and raise armies for the Vietnamese revolution with the promise of future support in their own struggles once the war was over.

After discussing politics with the Vietnamese students, Saloth and his fellow students were inspired and eager to see a revolution under the KPP in Cambodia. However, Saloth understood that an indigenous revolution was not likely to occur without the help of the Vietnamese Communists. The Khmer movement was too small and could not rely on Cambodia's peasantry to participate in a Communist revolution. As historian Craig Etcheson explains, the homogeneity and the long-standing lifestyle of the people worked against revolutionary action: "The leisurely pace of traditional life was inherently conservative."[13] Additionally, 80 percent of Cambodia followed Theravadic Buddhism, which teaches that a person's station in life, rich or poor, powerful or powerless, reflects his or her actions from past lives. Therefore, people tended to accept inequity in power and wealth, because those who are powerful and rich are deemed deserving of it, and those who are powerless and poor are deemed not yet deserving of these rewards.

Most peasants believed that by suffering through this life and living well, a person would be reborn to a better station in the next life. However, revolution required action in *this* life. So, Saloth concluded, the Khmer revolution would have to be achieved through educating and motivating the peasantry to rise up as well as to assault the existing power structure of the French and the Cambodian monarchy.

Some historians argue that even at this early stage Saloth in fact distrusted the Vietnamese. There is no direct evidence that Saloth was xenophobic or prejudiced against the Vietnamese at this

Buddhist monks pose at an ancient Cambodian temple. Approximately 80 percent of Cambodians followed the religion of Theravedic Buddhism.

time; however, he was certainly duplicitous in his relations with the Vietnamese Communists in the 1970s while he was in power. Other historians argue that his animosity toward the Vietnamese grew in the intervening decades because of disputes and conflicts. Regardless of how he felt at the time, Saloth clearly understood that to achieve revolution in his own country, the KPP would need the help of the organized and armed Vietminh.

Meeting the KPP

The first known contact between the newly formed Khmer People's Party and the members of the radical Khmer Student Association occurred in 1951. Ieng Sary and Thiounn Mumm were sent to East Berlin as KSA delegates to attend the Berlin Youth Festival. The festival was a Soviet-backed political conference and, as Craig Etcheson writes, it was apparently very influential on the radical delegates: "[The festival] appears to have been a profoundly significant event in the history of the [Cambodian Communist] revolution."[14]

Details of the conference are not known, but when it was over, Ieng Sary came away convinced that the only way to achieve revolution in Cambodia was by overthrowing the government. When the group returned to Paris, Saloth and the rest of the students became more focused on action rather than political theory. They once and for all dismissed the possibility of a democratic resistance movement and focused on studying techniques of subversion and revolutionary organization.

Challenging the Monarchy

The recharged group of students had their first opportunity to target the monarchy. Back home in Cambodia, Sihanouk continued to thwart the Democrats, who maintained a majority in the National Assembly. In 1952 he again dissolved the assembly and ruled by decree. Further, he again delayed elections for a new body and named himself prime minister.

In response to Sihanouk's coup d'état, Saloth and the other radical Khmer students in France sided with the Democrats. Saloth, Keng, and Hou Yuon wrote an essay openly attacking the king and challenging the concept of monarchy. Published in a Phnom Penh newspaper, the essay's flagrant disrespect for the king shocked many people.

Sihanouk's coup drove several of the members of the student group to join the French Communist Party. Although they sympathized with the Democrats, Saloth and others saw that Sihanouk was unwilling to allow democracy to work. Between 1949 and 1952, almost all of the members of the radical leftist clique of the Khmer Student Association, including Saloth—but not Keng and Ieng—joined the FCP. It is unclear exactly when Saloth joined, but it was likely in mid- to late 1952 and arranged through Thiounn Mumm, the longest-standing party member of the group.

Students march during the 1950 Berlin Youth Festival, a Communist political conference that members of the Khmer Student Association attended.

Around this time, several of the radical Khmers lost their scholarships because of their political activities and affiliation with the FCP. Saloth was not one of them. It is possible that he joined the party late enough or had kept a low enough profile so as not to be noticed, but school records show no acknowledgment of his political activities, as they did for Ieng Sary and others. However, Saloth did lose his scholarship for academic reasons. He later explained, "As I neglected my studies, the authorities cut off my scholarship."[15] He flunked out of school in spring 1952.

Returning Home

Saloth remained in Paris for a few months with Ieng Sary and Son Sen, another KSA member who would become important to the Cambodian Communists. Then, out of money, Saloth returned home via Marseilles and Saigon aboard the *Jamaique.* Although he had not earned a degree—he was the only one among the group of students not even to possess a high school-level degree—it did not seem to matter to him. According to friends, he was eager to return home and take up the revolutionary struggle. He had left Cambodia a student with little direction; he returned as a highly motivated revolutionary.

Chapter Three

REVOLUTIONARY

When Saloth returned to Cambodia after studying in France, he became active in the Communist movement to oppose King Sihanouk. However, as Sihanouk's power and despotism grew, divisions within the Communist Party further weakened its cause. Eventually, Saloth was forced into hiding, first living a double life and then going underground.

Coming Home

Saloth arrived in Phnom Penh in January 1953, finding his home much changed and in political upheaval. Just before Saloth arrived home, King Sihanouk had declared martial law throughout the country after dissolving the Democrat-led National Assembly for a third time when it refused to grant the king special, extraconstitutional powers.

After returning home, Saloth spent a period of time at his brother Loth Suong's house, disguising his sympathies for the Vietminh's cause and his plans to join them, perhaps because he feared his brother would condemn his decision or perhaps he feared the French police. However, he enthusiastically told his brother about his summer in Yugoslavia and he praised the Soviet Union.

Joining the Maquis

Saloth told his brother that he planned to go in search of nationalist guerrilla forces in the countryside west of Phnom Penh; however, he in fact spent the next several months walking to the east, toward the Vietnam border. He arrived at a Vietminh encampment in August 1953 and presented himself to the Maquis (guerrillas), telling them that he was a member of the French Communist Party.

After they confirmed his membership in the party through connections in Hanoi and Paris, the Vietminh assigned Saloth to a headquarters camp in the Kompong Cham district, half of which was staffed with Vietminh soldiers and half with Khmer recruits. The Vietminh also inducted Saloth into the Indochinese Communist Party rather than the weaker Khmer People's Party, possibly because of his FCP affiliation.

Although the Vietminh actively recruited Khmer Communists, they treated them as subordinates, frequently giving them menial tasks such as carrying buckets of excrement from the latrines. Saloth was no exception; however, he also received political training. He learned how to organize and train recruits to the Communist cause, how to "work with the masses at the base, to build up the independence of committees at the village level, member by member," [16] according to one of the Vietminh.

When Saloth Sar returned home to Phnom Penh (pictured) in 1953, he found the capital city in a state of political upheaval.

Although Saloth had no combat expe- rience and did not speak Vietnamese, it became clear to the Vietminh that he could be useful because of his connections with various groups, including the Democrats, the members of the royal palace, and the French Communists. One Vietminh offi- cer also noted that he was eager to rise in the party, commenting that he was a "young man of average ability but with a clear desire for power."[17]

Tou Sammouth, whom Saloth had met in Paris, arrived at the camp and became Saloth's mentor. This relationship lasted for approximately nine years. Tou was a gifted orator with a Buddhist edu-

Sihanouk Revises the Constitution

The rigged elections of 1955 were a devastating blow to the Democrats and more evidence to Saloth Sar and the Cambodian communists that constitutional means of independence would not work. After these elections, Prince Sihanouk and his Sangkum Party took over the National Assembly, and Sihanouk usurped power from the new government by having the 1947 con- stitution revised to grant more power to the monarchy. As Marie Alexandrine Martin writes in Cambodia: A Shattered Society, *Sihanouk was able to force the changes through and thus shore up the power of the monarchy because of the public's apathy and fear.*

The prince first prepared a revision of the constitution, passed by the Sangkum's National Assembly. The revision was supported by the arrival of provincial delegations in Phnom Penh and the receipt of petitions signed by several hundred thousand persons. All these means of propaganda were part of the traditional power of leaders to manipulate the people. Significant changes are evident:

The king will thus choose and appoint the members of government. . . . The king will have the right to interpret the texts of the constitution in the last instance. . . . As a matter of fact, the constitution is bestowed by the king upon his people. Since the king is considered the father of the constitution, the task of interpretation log- ically reverts to him alone.

. . . Peasants simply endorsed—without understanding—all that was offered them because they hoped to keep the peace. The revision resulted from Sihanouk's desire to pro- tect royal power against the Democrats rather than to implement a reform to benefit the people. . . . Unwilling to be supplanted, criticized, or even advised, the prince preferred to take matters in hand from the beginning of his mandate.

Citizens of Hanoi await the arrival of Vietminh troops at the end of the First Indochina War. With its cession to Communist rule, Hanoi became a safe haven for many members of the Khmer People's Party.

cation and was no doubt, like Saloth's high school teacher Khran Siphan, a strong influence on Saloth's developing speaking and teaching skills.

The year Saloth spent in the Vietminh camp also helped him advance his position within the party beyond that of his associates who had more education and training. As David Chandler writes:

> By walking to the frontier and offering his services he stole the march on better qualified colleagues in France like Ieng Sary, Hou Yuon, and Thiounn Mumm and on radicals in Phnom Penh who were still uncertain about communism or unwilling to take risks. [18]

A New Political Climate

Indeed, Saloth was among the few of his fellow radicals from Paris to take up direct political action upon returning. His interest in entering the political struggle had much to do with the change in the political climate. In a ceremony in November 1953, Sihanouk announced the ascendance of the independent Kingdom of Cambodia and pledged a policy of neutrality, a position he knew to be popular. The maneuver made him Cambodia's most powerful political figure.

Furthermore, eight months after Sihanouk declared Cambodia's independence, the First Indochina War ended. Having suffered a humiliating loss at the battle of Dien Bien Phu, the French were willing to negotiate peace. The peace was made official at a conference in Geneva, Switzerland, in July 1954, marking the end of the eight-year conflict. The peace accord divided Vietnam into north and south at the seventeenth parallel and provided for free elections in both Cambodia and Vietnam in 1955 and 1956, respectively.

The Geneva Conference had severe repercussions for the Communists in Cambodia. The Vietnamese Communists agreed to withdraw from Cambodia and no recognition of the Khmer People's Party was made. While Laotian Maquis fighting with the Vietminh were given a chance to disarm or regroup to the north, no such provision was given for the Cambodian Communists. Suddenly abandoned by their allies who had promised to help them once the Vietnamese struggle was over, many gave up the struggle and returned home. More than one thousand other KPP members left for safety in Hanoi; many would remain there for fifteen years. Among this group was Saloth's former KSA associate Rath Sameourn. This loss severely diminished the KPP membership in Cambodia.

Splitting Ideologies

These major events in the political landscape in Indochina caused a split in ideologies among the former Khmer Student Association radicals about how to proceed with the struggle for revolution. Like many Communists, particularly members of the KPP, Saloth, Ieng Sary, and others from the group denied Cambodia's independence and felt that armed struggle

against what they saw as the despotic Sihanouk government must be the first priority of the revolution. Khieu Samphan, Hu Nim, Hou Yuon, and others argued that U.S. imperialism was the primary threat, because the United States was providing the French with billions of dollars to fight in Vietnam.

Those Cambodian Communists who remained in the country following the Geneva Conference included a small group of guerrillas, Saloth among them, working in remote regions with the remaining Vietminh. The rest of the Cambodian Communists, including Son Sen, Hu Nim, and Hou Yuon, remained above ground, working through various channels to influence the government. Even radical Ieng Sary went to work as a teacher at a private school Hou Yuon opened.

Preparing for the 1955 Elections

Regardless of their location or position, Saloth and his fellow Communists were hopeful for a Democratic victory in the 1955 elections. Called for by the Geneva Conference, these elections were viewed as the first authentic elections of an independent Cambodia and were a high-stakes political event. Their outcome marked a turning point in the course of the country's history and in Saloth's life.

The groups competing for National Assembly seats included the progressive Democrats under Mumm and Keng, who had managed to take over the party leadership; the Indochinese Communist Party, which was fronted by an organization called the Pracheachon Group in order to hide its Communist affiliation; the centrist so-called Thanhist Democrats; the conservative Liberal Party; and various other anti-Democratic organizations, many of them sharing an allegiance to the king.

Of the parties contending, the most promising was the progressive Democrats. They were the best organized, had the largest number of followers, were the only ones with a clear national platform, and were seen as a balanced alternative to the Vietnamese-dominated Communists and the Sihanouk regime.

In October 1954 Saloth returned to Phnom Penh. Keng and Mumm sought him out, hoping he could help with the election. They found him living under an assumed name in the southern part of the city, no doubt afraid that if his ICP affiliation was discovered, he would be arrested.

Saloth helped Keng and Mumm by working as a liaison between their party and the Communists, although he never revealed to his colleagues that he was a member of the ICP. It is likely, in fact, that Tou Sammouth had sent him to the capital to try to radicalize the Democrats and

French soldiers capture a Vietminh guerrilla during the First Indochina War. After the war ended in 1954, Saloth believed only armed struggle could bring about lasting change.

to promote the cause of the Pracheachon Group as well.

With Keng, Saloth worked to help educate the electorate and to try to unite the various groups who opposed Sihanouk. This meant trying to bridge the gaps between those who were willing to work with the Vietnamese Communists and those who were not, as well as between those who wanted to reform the government and those, like himself, who eventually wanted to overthrow it.

During his efforts in the election preparations, Saloth was joined again by Khieu Ponnary, who had returned from Paris in 1951 and had taken a job teaching Cambodian literature at a high school in the capital. It is likely that their romantic relationship began at this time if it had not already.

Sihanouk and the Sangkum

Saloth and the other progressive Democrats were no doubt optimistic as the elections approached. Most expected that the Democrats would win handily, as they had in previous elections. However, in March 1955, King Sihanouk shocked the nation, including his own parents, when he abdicated the throne to his father, Norodom Suramarit, in order to run for office as a private citizen.

Sihanouk—now Prince Sihanouk—then formed a political party called Sangkum Reastr Niyum (meaning Popular Socialist Community) and set in motion an aggressive and often violent campaign. Although a private citizen, he used his

royal influence over the police and military to compel enrollment in his party and to damage the Democrats. Although Saloth avoided injury, police and soldiers attacked opposition party members. Many Democrats were beaten, and some campaign workers were killed. In the midst of this violence, Keng Vannsak was arrested and Thiounn Mumm fled to France.

In 1955 King Sihanouk abdicated the throne to his father, Norodom Suramarit (pictured).

A Position of Moral Authority

During the late 1950s and early 1960s, Saloth Sar taught at a politically radical private school, Chamraon Vichea in Phnom Penh. As David P. Chandler writes in his book, The Tragedy of Cambodian History: Politics, War, and Revolution Since 1945, *Saloth was a popular teacher who, like other Communist teachers, used his influence and position of moral authority to encourage his students to join the party.*

A radical reputation also clung to Chamraon Vichea (Progressive Study) school . . . [where] Saloth Sar taught geography, history, civics, and French literature . . . between 1956 and 1963. Two of his former students remember him with affection. One, the novelist and editor Soth Polin, who studied French literature briefly under Sar in 1958–59, noted that Sar's teaching manner was genteel, almost unctuous. . . . Another student who . . . studied history with Sar in 1960 . . . recalled that he was "very popular with students and very correct in his ways." . . .

[A] student at another school . . . recalled him as being . . . "the kind of person whom you knew it would be easy to make friends with.". . .

In Cambodian culture the role of the teacher . . . and the student-teacher relationship have always been important in ethical, social, and intellectual terms. . . . [T]he knowledge imparted by . . . teachers and the bonds that developed between teachers and students often shaped the students' political attitudes. . . . By the late 1960s, when a Communist-led rebellion had broken out in much of Cambodia, many guerrilla bands were made up in part of former teachers and their students who had followed them into the forest.

When the elections were held in September 1955, people were intimidated at the polls. Thus the elections produced the results Sihanouk had hoped—the Sangkum swept the elections, winning all ninety-one seats in the National Assembly with 83 percent of the total votes.

Double Life

Sihanouk's victory in 1955 severely set back the opposition movements. Sihanouk used the rigged elections as a mandate to direct the Sangkum National Assembly and govern as he pleased. Cambodian Communists like Saloth had the choices of going underground, seeking exile in Hanoi, allying with Sihanouk, or committing to publicly opposing him. None of these choices appealed to Saloth and his group of radicals, but several of his friends chose to work in the open while keeping their Communist affiliations a secret.

Khieu Samphan, recently returned from Paris with a PhD, set up a French-language newspaper; Son Sen, Hu Nim, and Hou Yuon joined the Sangkum Party in order to be able to hold legitimate office.

Saloth, Ieng Sary, Khieu Ponnary, and others chose to engage in a double life. Saloth and Khieu married in 1956 on July 14, Bastille Day. The French national holiday, commemorating the storming of the Bastille prison in 1789 and marking the beginning of the French Revolution, was a significant choice for the two revolutionaries.

Like Khieu and Ieng, Saloth had a legitimate job as a teacher yet worked secretly with the ICP and KPP. Saloth was drawn to teaching because it allowed him to use his respected position to recruit young people into the Communist struggle.

Saloth took a job at Chamraon Vichea high school in Phnom Penh, which was designed for students who, like him, had not been able to pass the exams required to enter Lycée Sisowath. His years in Paris had given him an excellent background in French literature, and he also taught history, geography, and civics. As it turned out, he was also a talented, inspiring, and popular teacher whom students found to be honest, friendly, and eloquent. One student later recalled his delivery of lectures as "gentle and musical. . . . He spoke in bursts without notes, searching a little but never caught short, his eyes half-closed, carried away by his own lyricism."[19]

The recruits to the Communists were few at the time, most brought to the party by teachers like Saloth and his wife. Those attracted to the party between the years 1954 and 1960 were mostly students, teachers, and urban workers. Many were admirers of the Chinese revolution and did not like Sihanouk's dictatorial style.

Working for the Communists was dangerous during the period following the 1955 elections, so Saloth and his comrades met clandestinely and worked under cover, using passwords and pseudonyms. For the first time, Saloth began using the alias Pol (without Pot). The work consisted of bringing in recruits, educating and training them in party doctrine and policies, and forming networks of communication and organization.

Rising in the Party

Most of Saloth's party activities between 1955 and 1960 remain unknown. However, in September 1960, he was one of twenty-one delegates at a secret meeting of Cambodian Communists, called the Khmer Communist Party Congress, which took place over three days in an abandoned railway station in Phnom Penh. Others there included Tou Sammouth and Ieng Sary.

At the meeting, the congress decided to support the Vietnamese Communists with their plan to invade South Vietnam. The congress also restated its allegiance to Marxist-Leninist policies, assigned new responsibilities and officers, and changed the name of the organization to reflect a nominal independence from its ICP origins. Now called the Workers Party of Kampuchea (WPK) (Kampuchea being the Khmer name for the country), it was to be led by Tou Sammouth, who became the secretary general. The deputy secretary position went to Nuon Chea, a young Communist who had worked with the Vietminh, and third in the line of power was Saloth, who served as Tou's assistant.

A Formidable Opponent

Despite the policy adopted by the Communist congress, Saloth and Ieng remained convinced that the party should focus on overthrowing Sihanouk rather than aiding the Vietnamese Communists with their struggle. Soon after the meeting, they secretly formed their own hard-line clique, which would eventually grow to include most of the members of the Pol Pot regime of the mid- to late 1970s.

As a young Communist, Saloth posed for a number of photos like this one that portrayed him as a man of the people.

Meanwhile, between the years 1960 and 1963, their number-one enemy, Prince Sihanouk, rose to the zenith of his power. Following his father's death, he was appointed head of state, the highest office in the land.

To avoid being drawn into the rising conflict between U.S. and South Vietnamese forces and the Vietminh and their affiliated National Liberation Front guerrilla forces in the south (also known as the Vietcong), Sihanouk used his power over the National Assembly to strike a careful balance of neutrality to appease both the Communist and anti-Communist powers at war. Sihanouk believed that Vietnam would prevail but also feared that a united Communist country next door would be a threat to Cambodian sovereignty. Thus he preached anti-Americanism while accepting U.S. military aid. Meanwhile, in the early 1960s, he began a violent crackdown on Communists within Cambodia while being careful not to antagonize foreign Communist forces, specifically those of China, North Vietnam, and its patron the Soviet Union.

Communists in Trouble

While Sihanouk worked to ingratiate himself with foreign Communist leaders by beginning diplomatic relations with China and the Soviet Union, he imprisoned suspected Communists or sympathizers who were still operating in the open in Cambodia. He also imprisoned

American troops disembark at the Mekong Delta during the Vietnam War. The U.S. and South Vietnamese conflict caused Cambodia's Prince Sihanouk to employ new political tactics.

the editors of leftist newspapers, including Khieu Samphan. His police and military went looking for Communists, whom Sihanouk began calling the Khmer Rouge (or Red Khmer), a name that would thereafter be used by those outside the party.

Between 1960 and 1962, the Cambodian Communists suffered several serious setbacks. First, a high-ranking party member was discovered to have been a spy for Sihanouk; his work caused massive damage to the organization and created an environment of distrust that nearly destroyed the party. Then, in 1962, Tou Sammouth disappeared and was presumed killed by Sihanouk's police or military, now under the leadership of General Lon Nol, the brother of Saloth's best friend from high school.

Tou's disappearance had ominous implications within the party. It was certain that someone within the party had given Sihanouk's government information on how to find him. In fact, many believe that Saloth himself was the informant, allegedly because Tou had a different political stance regarding Vietnam and possibly because Saloth wanted to gain promotion within the party. Others argue that there is no evidence that Saloth distrusted the Vietnamese as allies yet and therefore the motive makes no sense. Regardless, Saloth replaced Tou as acting secretary general and then assumed the position permanently in February 1963.

As the secretary general, Saloth gave numerous secret seminars to recruits or potential recruits. As eloquent and inspir-

As the army's chief of staff in the 1960s General Lon Nol (pictured) sought to rid Cambodia of enemies to the Sihanouk government.

ing in his seminars as he was in the classroom, he focused on the injustices of the Sihanouk government.

Into Hiding

Saloth's double life came to an end soon after he was made secretary general. In

In 1963 two bodies lie in a Phnom Penh street after police quelled a student riot. Saloth and other Communists were blamed for the riots.

early 1963, anti-Sangkum student protests against police harassment and brutality in the northwest city of Siem Reap, near the ancient capital of Angkor, turned into riots. Over the course of a few days, one student was killed and several were wounded. The violence spread as sympathy protests erupted in Phnom Penh and Kompong Cham.

The riots occurred while Sihanouk was out of the country, but he sent word back to General Lon Nol to investigate. Lon took the opportunity to crack down on Communists, whom he believed, probably correctly, had instigated the protests.

When he returned, Sihanouk approved Lon Nol's actions and then turned over a list of thirty-four suspected Communists and leftist subversives to Lon Nol with orders to arrest them. The names on the list included Ieng Sary, Son Sen, and Saloth. Their positions within the WPK were not likely known; however, they were teachers in schools known to be recruiting points for Communists.

In March 1963 Saloth, his wife, and Ieng decided to flee the capital to hide out in the remote jungle where the Vietminh still had bases. From there, he and his fellow Communists would regroup, recruit, and plan for the future.

Chapter Four

Rising to Power

In 1963 Saloth fled Phnom Penh to become a full-time revolutionary. For the next twelve years under his leadership, in the jungles and rural countryside, the Cambodian communists bided their time, making plans for the overthrow of the Sihanouk Sangkum government and for the Communist society they would attempt to build while amassing a large guerrilla army.

In 1968 the so-called Khmer Rouge communist forces took up armed struggle against the government, sparking a civil war that would last seven years. Unwittingly, divisions and a military coup within the Sihanouk government, as well as U.S. bombing and ground missions into Cambodia, created a climate in which the Cambodian communists under Pol Pot were able to obtain their long-awaited objective of revolution.

Office 100

When Saloth left the capital to escape Sihanouk's military and security forces under General Lon Nol, he returned east to take refuge with the Vietminh in a base in Kampong Cham near the Vietnamese border. The base, code-named Office 100, moved back and forth across the Cambodian-Vietnamese border as needed to avoid military assaults.

Saloth spent two years with the Vietminh and a few Khmer Communists, holding study meetings and making plans. Because of his situation, he was essentially hostage to the Vietnamese. He and the other Cambodians were forbidden to leave the base, and they were cut off from world events except for shortwave radio broadcasts from China and Vietnam. According to David Chandler, the period marked a low point in Saloth's career:

He accomplished little and "[f]or the next two years he chafed under humiliating Vietnamese protection."[20]

A Scolding from Vietnam

Saloth was able to leave the base in April 1965 when Le Duan, the Vietnamese Communist party leader, summoned him to Hanoi. Apparently, the leadership and

U.S. military involvement in Cambodia in the late 1960s and early 1970s inadvertently aided Pol Pot's rise to power.

the numerous Khmer Communists—many who had fled following the 1955 elections and others who had left Cambodia in the political turmoil since—wanted to meet the new secretary general of the WPK.

With his wife Saloth Ponnary and a former Pracheachon member and school-teacher Keo Meas, Saloth walked north through Cambodia toward Hanoi along the Ho Chi Minh Trail, a series of roads cutting through Laos and Cambodia used by the Vietnamese Communists to move supplies and personnel from the north to the south. Saloth was greatly impressed by the massive and constant movement of trucks along the road.

It took two months to walk to Hanoi, and when Saloth arrived, he suffered humiliating treatment from his hosts. Le Duan chastised Saloth for making trouble for Sihanouk—presumably referring to the recent riots—and for pursuing a Cambodian nationalist objective. According to a 1978 account by Saloth and other Cambodian communists, the Vietnamese insisted that Saloth's WPK "renounce revolutionary struggle and wait for Vietnamese to win their victory, which would automatically produce victory in Cambodia"; whereas the Vietnamese say they told Saloth to "support Sihanouk while criticizing him, and maintain a political but not military struggle."[21]

Although Saloth no doubt disagreed with Le—this advice was, as Craig Etcheson writes, "a recipe for political frustration or mass arrests,"[22]—the WPK

Ho Chi Minh's portrait sits atop a government building in Hanoi, North Vietnam. Saloth met with Communist leaders in Hanoi before visiting China in 1966.

was in no position to break from the Vietnamese, so he accepted the criticism.

Saloth stayed on in North Vietnam for several months while waiting for permission to visit China and meet with Mao Tse-tung and other leaders of the People's Republic of China. This meeting was important not only as a gesture of alliance between the WPK and the Chinese Communists but perhaps also as a strategic maneuver on Saloth's part. Following the death of Stalin in 1953, a gradually increasing split had occurred between the Soviets, now led by Secretary General Nikita Khrushchev, and Chinese Communists under Mao. The two leaders disliked each other personally and this difficulty led to serious political tensions between the countries. Since the Viet-

namese Communists were more closely allied with the Soviets, it is possible that Saloth wanted to take the opportunity to become friendly with the Chinese, who might later help him oppose the Vietnamese.

Meeting Mao

Saloth received permission to visit China in 1966 and traveled to Beijing. He arrived at a pivotal and energized moment in the history of the country. In 1966, seven years after the inauguration of the Great Leap Forward, Mao's disastrous agricultural revolution that had caused millions to die from famine, Mao had launched the Cultural Revolution, which intended to erase the past and reinvent Chinese culture. Millions of Chinese

New recruits into Mao's Red Guard applaud after being sworn in. The Red Guard was responsible for fostering cultural change throughout China.

youth had been recruited as Mao's Red Guard, charged with fostering and enforcing radical cultural changes throughout the country, often by force. Despite the ultimate failure of this plan, in 1966 Mao's cult of celebrity was on the rise, and Saloth, arriving in the midst of the revolution, was tremendously influenced by it and by Mao. During this visit, Saloth's loyalties shifted from the Vietnamese to the Chinese. As David Chandler writes, "The visit to China was a turning point in his career. Prudently, however, he said nothing to the Vietnamese about his change of heart."[23]

New Situations, New Strategies

Saloth returned to eastern Cambodia in late September 1966. While he was in China, the Second Indochina War, between the Vietnamese Communists and South Vietnam and its U.S. allies, had massively escalated.

Additionally, Sihanouk's position of neutrality on Vietnam had made him increasingly unpopular with his anti-Communist constituents, many of whom were in positions of power within the government. Believing the Communists would win, Sihanouk broke off diplomatic and aid relations with the United States that had been established soon after Cambodia's independence. By the 1966 elections, he had lost his support among and control over the National Assembly. During these elections, right-wing General Lon Nol became prime minister, signaling even more trouble for Saloth and the WPK.

In response to these and other developments and inspired by his visit to China, Saloth called a meeting to discuss new strategies and tactics for the future. However, the position of the Cambodian Communists was so impaired that the plans derived from the meeting were largely limited to regrouping and relocating. One of the first items on the agenda was again to rename the party, this time from the Workers Party of Kampuchea to the Communist Party of Kampuchea (CPK). Saloth's motives for the change are unclear, but some analysts suggest that it was a gesture to reassert his power over the organization and claim some symbolic independence from the Vietnamese.

Additionally, Saloth moved the party's base north, from Kompong Cham into the more remote district of Ratankiri. (By 1968 the base had been moved two more times within the region to avoid military assault.) On his way north in 1967, Saloth contracted malaria and had to be nursed back to health before moving on. But once in Ratankiri, he was joined by several other key members of his group, including Son Sen, Keo Meas, and Ieng Sary, at a compound code-named Office 104.

There, in the remote jungle, the Communists lived among the tribal minorities

of the country. These indigenous people lived off the land as hunter-gatherers, and because of years of infringement upon their lands by the French and then the Sihanouk government, they were willing to join the Communists to fight the Cambodian government.

Samlaut

As Saloth and the CPK/Khmer Rouge worked to gather strength and continued to plan for revolution, an uprising in the northwestern city of Battambang and the events that followed it sparked the fire that would lead them into armed conflict with the government.

In the mid-1960s much of Cambodia's rice harvest was smuggled into Vietnam to help support the Communist cause.

After the loss of U.S. military aid, the Sihanouk government began to rely more heavily on export taxes placed on rice production. The rice harvests of the early to mid-1960s had been record breaking; however, large portions of the crops were smuggled out of the country to supply the Vietnamese Communists without being taxed. To combat this, the government assigned armed security forces to collect taxes, and they frequently became violent.

In April 1967, when collectors became violent with farmers in a village near Battambang, they were attacked by peasants. More than two hundred peasants marched on an army post near Samlaut where they killed two soldiers and stole weapons.

Sihanouk was out of the country, and Prime Minister Lon Nol took extreme action. Believing that the riots were Communist-inspired, he sent soldiers and police in to viciously subdue the uprising. According to one critic, "The pacification of the disturbed region was undertaken with the rude vigor peculiar to a soldiery who had been promised a monetary reward for each severed head they might forward to military headquarters in Phnom Penh."[24]

When Sihanouk returned, he approved Lon Nol's actions and turned on left-wing activists and politicians in Phnom Penh, among them Khieu Samphan, Hu Nim, and Hou Yuon, who had become opposition members within Sihanouk's government. Like many who participated in the uprising, they and many other leftists fled into the countryside to join the CPK/Khmer Rouge.

The violence spread to other parts of the country, and everywhere the protests were met with violence. An estimated ten thousand peasants and supporters were killed. Although there is no direct evidence linking the Communists to the uprising, the revolt served a dual purpose for them: It provided thousands of new recruits for the CPK and it also convinced them that the only way forward was an armed struggle. Saloth later said, "If we did not take up armed struggle, we would be incapable of defending the revolutionary forces."[25]

In the months of violence through the end of 1967, Saloth and the CPK/Khmer Rouge planned their armed rebellion. Their largest problems were that they had few weapons with which to fight and their Communist allies—China, North Vietnam, and the Soviet Union—were not willing to help them wage war against Sihanouk.

Nonetheless, a military clash between Cambodian security forces and the CPK/Khmer Rouge on January 17, 1968, at Bay Damram was celebrated among the Communists as the birth of the new Revolutionary Army and the beginning of their armed revolution.

American Military Actions

Most important among any of the objectives Saloth and his group had at this point was the recruitment and training of soldiers. The number of members in the

A woman pleads with the photographer after she and her husband were caught in the crossfire of a battle between the CPK/Khmer Rouge and Cambodian security forces.

CPK/Khmer Rouge had climbed after the Samlaut rebellion but not enough to wage a sustained and victorious war on the Cambodian army. However, several events and forces aided the Communists in recruiting. Foremost among these were massive ground operations and aerial bombing campaigns launched by the U.S. government, ostensibly to destroy Vietnamese Communist bases within Cambodia's borders. Ordered by President Richard Nixon and long kept secret from the U.S. public and Congress, these actions killed an estimated six hundred thousand Cambodians and created untold numbers of refugees. However, rather than weakening the Communist presence in Cambodia, the destruction drove hundreds of thousands into the CPK/Khmer Rouge, both out of revenge and because many had

Operation Menu

On February 9, 1969, U.S. military intelligence reported the existence of a key Vietnamese Communist base a few miles inside the border of Cambodia. Military commanders persuaded U.S. president Richard Nixon to eliminate the base with a B-52 carpet-bombing attack (so called because the attack could decimate an area two miles by one-half mile). The mission was code-named Operation Breakfast in honor of the breakfast meeting at which Nixon approved the strike. And on March 9, 1969, the United States bombed approximately forty-eight square miles of Cambodian territory.

Over the course of the next fourteen months, the United States conducted 3,630 additional B-52 bombing raids over Cambodia, each major operation code-named following the theme of the first: Operations Lunch, Snack, Dinner, Dessert, and Supper. The White House kept all of the missions secret, fearing that the press would use them against the administration, which had promised to get the country out of the Vietnam War.

Despite months of air strikes, the bombings did not reduce Vietnamese Communist activities; in fact, more Communist forces moved deeper into Cambodia.

nowhere else to go. Many historians argue that were it not for these U.S. actions, Saloth would never have had the ability to take over the country. As Peter Hercombe notes, "Pol Pot can thank the Americans for his ticket to power."[26]

Overthrow of Sihanouk

Even with the forces amassing behind the CPK/Khmer Rouge in the late 1960s, the turning point in the civil conflict between the Phnom Penh government and the CPK/Khmer Rouge was the overthrow of Prince Sihanouk in 1970. On March 18, while Sihanouk was away on an official visit to Paris and Moscow, Lon Nol executed a coup d'état in Phnom Penh. Unhappy with Sihanouk's past appease-ment of the Communists, the National Assembly voted to grant full power over the government to Lon Nol and to arrest Sihanouk and charge him with treason if he returned to the country. Lon then declared a state of emergency and suspended numerous civil rights, allowing arrest without charge and banning public assembly.

Unwittingly, Lon Nol had done Saloth and the Cambodian Communist movement an enormous favor by deposing Sihanouk. The coup removed the country's foremost ally with China and North Vietnam, thus clearing the way for the two Communist countries to finally approve and support CPK/Khmer Rouge aggression against the Cambodian government.

More important, because of the coup, Sihanouk entered into a military alliance with his former enemies, under a group called the United Front, to fight for his return to power.

While the alliance was one of necessity for Sihanouk, it was one of convenience for Saloth and the CPK/Khmer Rouge. The Communists used Sihanouk as a figurehead to disguise their Communist agenda from the rest of the world and to increase their resistance force with those loyal to the prince.

Many thousands of Cambodians entered the CPK/Khmer Rouge in support of Sihanouk during this period, and Saloth spent much of his time indoctrinating the new members. Always a gifted teacher, he now turned his abilities toward propaganda, instilling in his recruits a deep hatred for the Americans, the South Vietnamese, and especially the Lon Nol government. The CPK/Khmer Rouge told peasants and refugees that the U.S. B-52 bombers that were destroying the country were based in the capital,

During a television address in 1970, President Richard Nixon announces that U.S. troops have been deployed in Cambodia to target Communist operations.

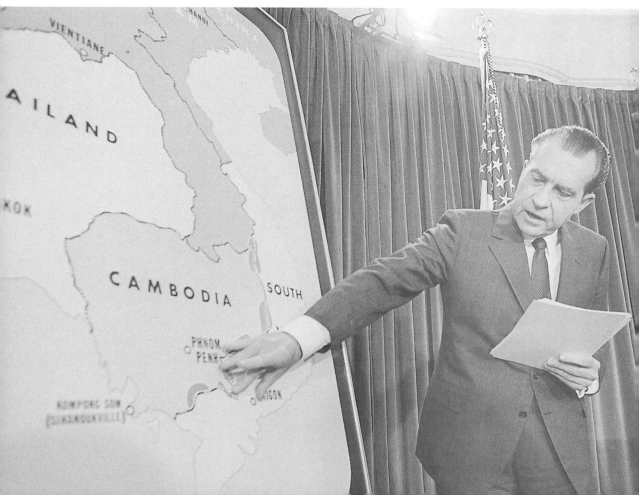

Phnom Penh, when in fact they were flown in from Guam and the Philippines.

Sihanouk Meets Saloth

Arrangements for the United Front organization had been made with Saloth's and Sihanouk's approval, but until 1973 the leaders had not met. Moreover, when they finally did meet, only one of them was aware of it.

Sihanouk secretly returned with his wife to Cambodia in February. Officially, he had disappeared after he left Beijing, but, in fact, he traveled along the Ho Chi Minh Trail from the Chinese border into Cambodia accompanied by Ieng Sary. Sihanouk was taken to Angkor, the historic Cambodian capital, under the con-

trol of the CPK/Khmer Rouge, where he met with top Communist Party members as a mutual show of support and strength. Among the CPK/Khmer Rouge were Saloth Ponnary (Saloth's wife), Khieu Samphan, Hou Yuon, Hu Nim, Ieng Sary, Son Sen, and Saloth. However, Saloth presented himself without revealing his status as secretary general.

The meeting was tense but covered in smiles and polite talk. Sihanouk and his wife were treated to music and theater, and the meetings were photographed and filmed as propaganda. However, as Chandler writes, "Nothing was as it appeared; no one could speak his mind. Everyone except for a handful of leaders was being observed, suspected, and used."[27]

On the Run

In the first year of the CPK/Khmer Rouge armed struggle against Sihanouk–Lon Nol forces, the CPK/Khmer Rouge allies had not supplied the insurgents with the armaments they needed. Greatly outgunned, the insurgents fought where they could but also spent a great deal of time on the run from security forces. In an interview given in the late 1970s, quoted in David P. Chandler's Brother Number One: A Political Biography of Pol Pot, *Saloth discussed the dire condition of the guerrilla forces in the early days of the civil war.*

In some areas where the enemy engaged the people, we were cut off. We lacked personnel. We had no economy. We had no military strength and nowhere to hide. No matter how big the forests were, we found no shelter. No matter how good the people were, the enemy squeezed and manhandled them, and they could do nothing. If people were not good, the enemy controlled and commanded them. The enemy knew the forests. Wherever we came and went, he was aware of us. We had a few weapons here and there, but we had no land and no people under our control.

Pushing Toward Phnom Penh

By the time Sihanouk made his visit to Angkor, U.S. involvement in the war in Vietnam was over. In January 1973, a peace agreement between the United States and the Vietnamese Communists officially ended the war. The last U.S. troops pulled out of Vietnam that year, but fighting between North and South reerupted in 1974. In the three years since Lon Nol's coup against Sihanouk, the Cambodian army had suffered massive losses fighting alongside American and South Vietnamese troops against the Vietcong on the Vietnamese border as well as the CPK/Khmer Rouge insurgents at home. With the weakening of Lon Nol's army, the CPK/Khmer Rouge made significant advances toward Phnom Penh. However, in late 1974, as the fall of Saigon to the Vietnamese Communists became imminent, most of their troops retreated from Cambodia, leaving the CPK/Khmer Rouge troops to fight alone.

Despite this setback, Saloth believed that victory was near. The CPK/Khmer Rouge continued to push toward Phnom Penh. By late March 1975, it was clear that the Communists had won. On April 1, 1975, Lon Nol abandoned Phnom Penh for the United States, and evacuations of foreigners and embassies followed. Two weeks later, the CPK/Khmer Rouge forces entered the capital with little resistance. The revolution was a success, and after two decades of planning, Saloth was poised to lead the country.

Chapter Five

Ruler in the Shadows

With the success of the Communist revolution in Cambodia, Saloth Sar became the leader of the newly formed country of Democratic Kampuchea. For the first two years he remained invisible, guiding from behind the anonymity of the revolutionary government, called Angkar. From the beginning, Saloth Sar sought to radically change every aspect of life in Cambodia, shifting it toward his ideal of a Communist utopia.

The "Glorious Revolution"

The 1975 Communist takeover of the Cambodian capital, Phnom Penh, occurred on April 17, which coincided with the traditional Cambodian New Year. Many people were celebrating in the streets when various factions of the CPK/Khmer Rouge entered the city. Since 1970, refugees fleeing violence from the civil war in the coun-

tryside had sought shelter in the city, and the population had swelled to 2–3 million people. The capital had fallen easily, weakened by the war for months, even years. According to journalist Edward S. Herman: "When the Khmer Rouge took over . . . the country was shattered, starvation and disease were already rampant—8,000 people a day were dying in Phnom Penh alone."[28]

In the capital, the war-weary people turned out to give the soldiers heroes' welcomes. Their capture of the city meant that the long and harsh civil war was over. However, many in the city did not understand that the CPK/Khmer Rouge soldiers, most of them young, with unsmiling faces, clad in the peasant garb of black pajamas, were not there to rescue the population.

Along with his cadre of CPK/Khmer Rouge leaders, Saloth Sar—who at this time took his revolutionary pseudonym Pol Pot—had indoctrinated the CPK/Khmer Rouge peasant soldiers to hate their fellow Cambodians who had not joined the revolution. The soldiers had been taught to look upon everyone outside the revolution as subhuman, as parasites. These people were called "new people" or "April 17 people," because they had not joined the revolution until the "glorious revolution" forced them to do so.

Executions and Evacuations

On orders from Pol Pot, the first thing the soldiers did once they had secured Phnom Penh was to force the complete evacuation of the major cities and towns. To encourage cooperation, they lied, announcing that the Americans were going to bomb the cities and that people had to take refuge in the country. The soldiers encouraged people to leave their homes unlocked, telling them that they would take care of

Soldiers of the CPK/Khmer Rouge parade through the streets of Phnom Penh on April 17, 1975, signaling an end to Cambodia's long and bloody civil war.

the dwellings and that people would be able to return home in two or three days. This was also a lie. Pol Pot organized forced labor camps in the countryside where people, no matter what their skills or former station in society, were compelled to take up menial labor such as farming.

This woman fell victim to the CPK/Khmer Rouge's assault on Phnom Penh.

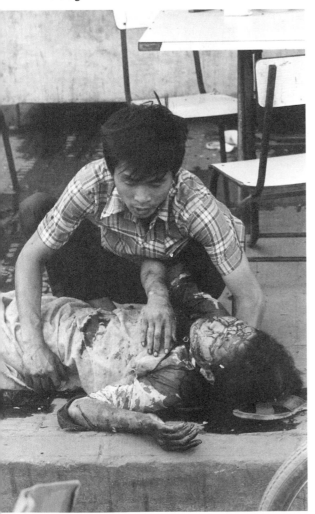

Those who refused to evacuate their homes were threatened with having their houses blown up or with being shot. No exceptions were made in the evacuation because Pol Pot believed that he and his fellow leaders would not be safe unless the cities were completely cleared. Even ill or wounded patients in hospitals were forced out. Within three days, the only people who remained in Phnom Penh were soldiers and a few foreign diplomats and journalists who holed up in the French embassy. These people were soon removed from the country, taken to the Thai border in trucks.

The mass exodus created great hardship. Family members were separated from one another, many never to reunite. Although the CPK/Khmer Rouge provided some food for the evacuees, it was nowhere near enough, and an estimated eleven thousand people died in the first few weeks from starvation, disease, lack of shelter from harsh weather, and exhaustion.

Still others were executed. Soldiers from Lon Nol's army, other Khmer Rouge security forces, and even bureaucrats were rounded up, taken out of sight, and shot. The CPK/Khmer Rouge killed civilians as well. Government workers, teachers, doctors, and other educated intellectuals and professionals were arrested and then taken out of sight and executed. The soldiers had been taught by the party that such people were a threat to the revolution: They represented antirevolutionary, procapitalist values and had been corrupted by the imperialists.

Evacuating Phnom Penh

Quoted in François Pouchard's book on the Pol Pot regime, Cambodia: Year Zero, *a young Cambodian man named Suon Phal, who was nineteen years old when the CPK/Khmer Rouge took over Phnom Penh, describes his experience of the evacuation of the capital.*

My family and I left the city and took the road to Prek Phneuv. Along the way I saw Khmer Rouge soldiers waiting in groups of three or four; they searched people and took their watches, radios, glasses, gold, and precious stones. Some even took 500-riel [Cambodian currency] bills and threw them in the air, saying, "The revolutionary Angkar has put an end to money." We had great difficulty making any headway because of the enormous crowd leaving town and also because some Khmer Rouge kept firing shots to scare us. Many people died on that march: the hospital patients who had been driven out, the women who gave birth on the road, the war casualties. We reached Vat Kak on April 25; along the way we saw many dead bodies scattered about everywhere—even in the pagodas—and the stench that came from them was almost unbearable.

Angkar

Pol Pot believed that the revolution was opposed by many and that there were enemies—even agents from the U.S. Central Intelligence Agency (CIA)—everywhere amidst the people. Thus, as Craig Etcheson writes, Pol Pot ordered evacuations in part for security reasons: "It would be very difficult to secure the cities against various counterrevolutionary elements, including the defeated military, foreign agents, and 'depraved' and 'traitorous' social elements."[29] Once the capital was evacuated, it was safe for the leadership to enter. Pol Pot arrived secretly on April 24, 1975.

On April 27, Khieu Samphan announced the formation of a new government called Democratic Kampuchea as an "independent, peaceful, neutral, sovereign, non-aligned Cambodia with territorial integrity."[30]

Publicly, it was announced that the new government would be headed by Sihanouk as chief of state, encouraging the illusion to foreign nations that the revolution had been to return the legitimate leadership of the king to power.

However, in truth, from the start Sihanouk was a puppet and effectively a prisoner of the CPK/Khmer Rouge leaders, who used his name and position to hide behind. Unlike Communist revolutions of the past in Russia and China, the Pol Pot regime did not reveal its Communist affiliation or even the identity of

This photo of Pol Pot (left) and Sihanouk was taken in the royal palace at Phnom Penh. Sihanouk was held under house arrest at the palace during Pol Pot's regime.

the revolutionary leaders. Pol Pot and the other leading members of the CPK/Khmer Rouge kept a low profile, and for two years their identities would remain virtually unknown. Internally it became known that the government was run by the supreme leadership of the party—also called the revolutionary organization, or Angkar—which, people were told, was faceless, nameless, and all-seeing.

Among the members of Angkar was Pol Pot, also known as Brother Number One; Nuon Chea, who was Brother Number Two; and Ieng Sary, Brother Number Three. Additionally it included Khieu Samphan, Son Sen, Saloth Ponnary,

Ieng Thirith, and others who had formed the inner circle of Saloth's associations since his years in Paris.

Policies of Angkar

The first major political conference of the new Democratic Kampuchean government was held in late May 1975, presided over by Pol Pot and his group. Although Pol Pot maintained his anonymity and did not emerge as the clear leader, the agenda of the meeting was his. It was an assembly of CPK/Khmer Rouge leaders from all over the country. Representatives from each district and region were required to attend, resulting in a crowd of several thousand, amassed at a sports stadium in Phnom Penh.

The purpose of the meeting was to announce the new regime's radical philosophies and policies. Perhaps the most radical philosophy was the elimination of Cambodian history. The revolution marked "Year Zero." People were to forget about the past, which Pol Pot believed had been corrupted. Additionally, Angkar ordered an eight-point policy to wipe out imperialism, religion, and enemies and to encourage collective labor and organization. These eight points are listed below:

1. Evacuate people from all towns.

2. Abolish markets.

3. Abolish the Lon Nol regime currency and withhold the revolutionary currency that had been printed.

4. Defrock all Buddhist monks and put them to work growing rice.

5. Execute all leaders of the Lon Nol regime, beginning with the top leaders.

6. Establish high-level cooperatives throughout the country with communal eating.

7. Expel the entire Vietnamese minority population from the country.

8. Dispatch troops to the border, particularly the Vietnamese border.

The last two of these points emphasized Pol Pot's belief that, despite their early assistance in the civil war against the Sihanouk and Lon Nol governments, the Vietnamese were as much an enemy to the revolution as was the United States or France. When this idea took root is highly debated, but an antagonistic foreign policy toward Vietnam was established from the beginning of the new government. In fact, clashes between Khmer and Vietnamese troops occurred within days of the government takeover.

Internally, the policies of Pol Pot and Angkar reshaped almost every aspect of Cambodian life. The population of new people was effectively enslaved. They were worked hard and mercilessly, and guards and leaders told them repeatedly "to keep you is no gain, to destroy you is no loss."[31] Further, education, money, and religion were abolished, as was the wearing of bright clothing, because it reflected individuality. Friendships were forbidden, forced marriages occurred, and children were separated from their mothers to be raised communally by Angkar. The people were told that Angkar was their only family.

New people in the countryside were set to work planting rice. Peter Hercombe says that this was Pol Pot's method of "purification from the contamination of urban life . . . through the nobility of physical life, through the contact with sacred Khmer earth."[32] Many urban people were unsuited for such labor and died from the hardship. Others were beaten or starved to death.

Members of Angkar

Behind the anonymity of the party, also known as Angkar, the innermost leaders of the Pol Pot regime included people Pol Pot had studied with in Paris in the 1950s. Additionally, others, such as Nuon Chea, Ta Mok, and Kang Khek Leu played equally important roles in the leadership. Here they are listed according to their duties in the regime.

Name	Position	Note
Pol Pot (Saloth Sar); aka Brother Number One	CPK secretary general; prime minister of DK	
Nuon Chea; aka Brother Number Two	CPK deputy secretary general; president of DK's People's Representative Assembly; DK Minister of the Interior (briefly served as prime minister in 1975)	
Ieng Sary (real name Kim Trang); aka Brother Number Three	CPK Central Committee member; DK deputy prime minister in charge of foreign affairs	
Khieu Samphan	President of Khmer Rouge	
Saloth Ponnary (formerly Khieu Ponnary); aka Sister Number One	President of DK's women	First wife of Saloth Sar/Pol Pot
Ieng Thirith (formerly Khieu Thirith)	Leader of DK youth groups	Wife of Ieng Sary
Ta Mok; aka The Butcher; aka Brother Number Seven	Southwest regional secretary; military commander of DK	Led evacuation of Phnom Penh
Son Sen	DK defense minister; chief aide to Pol Pot in 1990s	Executed under order of Pol Pot in 1998
Kang Khek Leu; aka Duch	DK minister in charge of S-21 prison	
Yun Yat	DK minister in charge of information and education (1975–1976); information minister (1977–1979)	Wife of Son Sen; executed under order of Pol Pot in 1998
Hu Nim	DK information minister	Executed in 1977 for challenging Angkar policy

Further, the country became completely isolated from the outside world. As Ben Kiernan writes:

In an era of mass communications, Cambodia was silent, sealed off. . . . Borders were closed, foreign embassies and press agencies expelled, newspapers and television stations shut down, radios confiscated, mail and telephone use suppressed, the speaking of foreign languages punished. [33]

Treatment at the hands of the CPK/ Khmer Rouge was not universally vicious but varied from village to village and region to region. The brutality against new people was worst where most directly influenced by Angkar, in the north and northwest. In the southwestern and eastern zones, treatment was often more fairhanded, if not less strict.

Government

Most of 1975 was consumed with administrative paperwork and bureaucratic duties as Pol Pot launched his new policies. Much of the country had been left in ruins by the war and rebuilding the nation required a great deal of planning and organization. One party member recalled the long hours that Pol Pot worked: "The whole day was full of work. Sometimes it went overtime. Generally at night it went on until eleven or twelve, and sometimes until one in the morning."[34]

The government of Democratic Kampuchea was officially launched in January

A long line of refugees enters Thailand as they flee the brutal repression of the Pol Pot regime.

1976 when a new constitution—Cambodia's third since 1953—was promulgated and the country's new name was made official. The constitution emphasized collectivization of labor and material resources, including orchards, fields, factories, farms, trains, automobiles, and sea craft. Only clothing, tools, and a few personal items remained private property. Additionally, the constitution provided for a new 250-seat legislature, called the People's Representative Assembly, for which elections were held on March 20 to fill its seats with party-selected candidates drawn from laborers, peasants, and members of the Revolutionary Army.

Sihanouk's position in the government became increasingly tenuous. Pol Pot realized that he no longer needed Sihanouk but felt he had to keep him quiet. Sihanouk was allowed to step down from his position as chief of state and then was placed under house arrest on the grounds of the royal palace in the capital.

Pol Pot publicly became Cambodia's prime minister in 1976 after Sihanouk officially resigned from office.

With Sihanouk no longer a figurehead for the government, Pol Pot was appointed to the position of prime minister in May 1976. His prerevolutionary identity was hidden, and Pol Pot was described as a rubber plantation worker with a peasant background.

Four-Year Plan

Shortly after his appointment as prime minister, Pol Pot visited China where he met with Mao Tse-tung, whom Saloth had admired. The Chinese leader advised his protégé against trying to replicate in Cambodia what Mao had attempted in China. "You should not completely copy China's experience, and you should think for yourself,"[35] Mao told him.

Nevertheless, Pol Pot strived for a goal similar to that of Mao's Great Leap Forward: the complete and rapid transformation to a Communist utopian collective where people would live and work for the good of the country and the party and not for personal gain. In fact, he planned his leap to be even more aggressive and rapid than Mao's had been. The results were even more disastrous.

Like Mao's Great Leap Forward, which resulted in famine and the starvation of an estimated 30 million people, Pol Pot's Four-Year Plan was an agrarian strategy to boost agricultural production and use the profits from the surplus to industrialize. However, Pol Pot's plan was even more incompetent and hastily constructed than Mao's had been. It sought to triple agricultural production within a year with-

Mao Tse-tung (left) greets Ieng Sary (right) and Pol Pot. Pol Pot tried to apply Mao's social and agricultural programs in Cambodia, with disastrous results.

out the benefit of modern machinery or tools and without any attention paid to the reality of the condition of the country. Although the plan was never fully implemented, even in its early stages it resulted in the country's first instance of mass starvation in over a century. Untold tens of thousands of people reportedly died during this period.

Enemies Within

Despite the clear failure of Pol Pot's plan, he refused to acknowledge fault. As one CPK/Khmer Rouge officer later said, he could not recognize his own errors: "Pol Pot took himself for a genius in every field. He thought he was a specialist in everything. For him everything was simple, everything was easy to realize. He stayed in an ivory tower cut off from reality, cut off from the people." [36]

Rather than accept the failure, Pol Pot blamed "hidden enemies, burrowing from within." [37] He believed that there were counterrevolutionaries and spies who were undermining his great plans, and he sought to eliminate them.

In Pol Pot's mind, the two worst enemies of the revolution were U.S. imperialism and an invasion by Vietnam. He

Survivor's Story

In his book A Cambodian Prison Portrait: One Year in the Khmer Rouge's S-21, *Vann Nath, one of the few inmates of the infamous S-21 prison to survive, writes a first-person account of his internment there, including this passage.*

After living [on two or three spoonfuls of rice a day] for several days my body began to deteriorate. My ribs were poking out and my body was like an old man of 70. My hair was overgrown like bamboo roots, and had become a nest for lice. I had scabies all over my body. My mind and spirit had flown away. I only knew one thing clearly: Hunger. Every four days, they gave us a bath. They brought hoses up from downstairs and sprayed everyone from the doorway. If you were on the far side of the room, like I was, you didn't get very wet.

Each day they would take some prisoners out of my room to be interrogated. They would handcuff and blindfold the prisoners before they left the room. Sometimes some of the prisoners came back with wounds or blood on their bodies, while others disappeared. Prisoners who had been there when I arrived started dying in the room, one by one. If a prisoner died in the morning, they would not take him out until night.

was particularly concerned with Vietnamese influence over the population, believing that there were people in his midst who had "Khmer bodies with Vietnamese minds."[38]

Secrecy became the number-one priority of Pol Pot. Further, he feared assassination so much that he surrounded himself with bodyguards, had food tested for poison, and refused to sleep in the same place twice. As his fear turned to paranoia, he came to mistrust almost everyone, and this led him to order the arrest, torture, and execution of thousands of Khmer, eventually to include members of the party and even close friends and associates.

S-21

Executions had begun as early as 1975, within the first months following the revolution. At that time Pol Pot created a secret police force called the Santebal and a special prison for the torture and interrogation of suspected enemies of the revolution. Housed in the former high school Tuol Svay in Phnom Penh, the secret prison was code-named S-21. The true nature of what happened in the buildings was known only to high-ranking Angkar officials and those who were imprisoned or worked there, but it soon gained an eerie reputation. One nearby factory worker called it "the place where people went in but never came out."[39]

Run by security head Kang Kech Leu, also known as Duch, and his boss, Son Sen, who was in charge of the Santebal (both of whom, like Saloth, had been schoolteachers), S-21 was the site of horrific abuse. It combined the functions of incarceration, investigation, adjudication, and counterespionage. People were rounded up and imprisoned there based on the slightest suspicion of being subversive or for deviating from the strict codes of behavior laid out by Angkar. Once there, prisoners were housed alone in either tiny individual cells or large classrooms with masses of others. In either case, prisoners were shackled to the floor, given paltry rations of food, were forbidden from talking, and were subject to sometimes daily interrogations, which always included torture such as electric shock, suffocation, beatings, and other physical and psychological abuse.

Killing Fields

The procedures for torture and interrogation were systematic and intended to extract confessions of guilt from prisoners. Each person brought to the prison

Clothes taken from inmates at S-21 prison are piled up to the ceiling in the interrogation room. Inmates of the prison were subjected to horrific tortures.

was considered guilty upon arrival and expected to confess their guilt. The confessions were to include lists of others who were guilty of subversion or counterrevolutionary activity. Under the duress and pain of torture, people regularly falsified confessions, often listing the names of whomever they could think of as long as it would end the torture. These confessions, which were turned over to Pol Pot, were the ultimate goal of S-21.

Once prisoners had provided interrogators with a confession, they were secretly taken out of the prison in trucks in the middle of the night to a former orchard at Choeung Ek. There they were bludgeoned to death and their bodies were thrown into a pit. An estimated seventeen thousand to twenty thousand people were killed there between 1975 and 1978. Numerous other such mass burial sites existed all over the country for the same purpose. These sites came to be called the Killing Fields. Pol Pot would later deny any knowledge of S-21 and the Killing Fields, but it is clear to most historians that their ultimate purpose was to satisfy Pol Pot's paranoia over security.

Although most of those taken to S-21 were young Khmer men, the population included women and sometimes children. When a man was imprisoned for what was euphemistically called reeducation, his wife and children were frequently taken along. Males and females were housed and interrogated separately, but women were separated from their children and frequently were sexually abused by the young guards. When the men were taken to Choeung Ek for execution, their families were also taken to be killed. One former guard explained that even women and children prisoners were seen as the enemy and were abused and executed mercilessly.

> When the Party makes an arrest, it arrests an enemy of the Party. If we arrest the husband, we arrest the wife and children too. Even our own parents or brothers or sisters. If the Party arrests them, they're enemies. . . . If we were ordered to destroy them, we did. The Party never made a mistake. [40]

Many of the guards later claimed they committed abuses and murder because they feared for their own lives. One said, "I realized that I was really a prisoner there, too. When I heard people scream, I was worried that, if I did anything, they would torture and kill me." [41]

Revolution Feeding on Its Own Children

In addition to perpetuating fear and inhumanity within the new revolutionary country, the arrests and executions eventually turned the party on itself. In late 1976 Pol Pot began to indicate that the enemies were not limited to counterrevolutionaries among the populace but people within his own party. Since the success of the revolution, the party continued to grow by the hundreds. However, Pol Pot was suspicious, trusting only a few longtime friends and

Rules of Imprisonment

Reprinted in Boreth Ly's article "Devastated Vision(s): The Khmer Rouge Scopic Regime in Cambodia" in the Spring 2003 issue of Art Journal, *the following "Ten Security Regulations" were written for prisoners and found posted outside one of the buildings on the S-21 prison compound.*

1. You must answer accordingly to . . . questions. Don't turn them away.
2. Don't try to hide the facts by making pretexts about this and that. You are strictly prohibited to contest [orders].
3. Don't be a fool, for you are a man who dares to thwart the [R]evolution.
4. You must immediately answer my questions without wasting time to reflect.
5. Don't tell . . . about either your immoralities or the essence of the Revolution.
6. While getting lashes or electrification you must not cry at all.
7. Do nothing, sit still, and wait for my orders. If there is no order, keep quiet. When [asked] to do something, you must do it right away without protesting.
8. Don't tell . . . how much you hate people from Kampuchea Krom in order to hide your Vietnamese ancestry.
9. If you don't follow the rules above, you shall get many lashes of the electric wire.
10. If you disobey any point of [the] regulations, you will get either ten or five electrical shocks.

members of Angkar—and even those he was not entirely certain about. He soon came to believe that there were spies in the party. He spoke of them as a sickness that had to be routed out: "The sickness is seeping into every corner of the Party, the army and among the people."[42]

In late 1976 and early 1977, Pol Pot began purges of party members. They were arrested and interrogated at S-21. Among these were the deputy minister for the economy and two zone secretaries, all three of whom had intimately known Pol Pot since the 1950s.

While these purges did in fact likely do away with a number of Pol Pot's internal enemies, they also greatly weakened the party through creating fear and mistrust and robbing Angkar of some of its most capable members. As Craig Etcheson states:

The Khmer Rouge's best thinkers, best theorists, most dedicated cadre, best warriors, best revolutionaries, fell victim to these increasingly paranoid internal purges. In a very real sense, the revolution began to feed on its own children.[43]

Dozens of mass graves were dug on the S-21 prison compound to accommodate the thousands of people who fell victim to Pol Pot's murderous regime.

Further, the interrogations and confessions of ordinary Cambodian citizens as well as purged party members only served to reinforce Pol Pot's fear and paranoia. The confessions led to lists of subversives, which led to more arrests, more tortures, and more lists. The reports of the confessions stacked up on Pol Pot's desk, convincing him that the party and the country were rife with spies and enemies, particularly Vietnamese ones.

Pol Pot's paranoia and mistrust of Vietnam became increasingly consuming. It would eventually destroy the revolutionary government of Democratic Kampuchea, taking with it many more hundreds of thousands of people.

Chapter Six

BROTHER NUMBER ONE

During the three and a half years that Pol Pot spent as leader of Democratic Kampuchea, his concerns and his policies were dominated by the rising conflict with Vietnam. This conflict was fueled primarily by Pol Pot's regime, and despite the numerous chances to change the course of events, Pol Pot moved the country headlong into a misguided, direct conflict against a better-armed and better-trained army.

The conflict had repercussions throughout the regime. The citizenry experienced increased hardships and the number of purges of suspected enemies rose. Additionally, the conflict caused Pol Pot to finally reveal his leadership to the public and to open the country to visitors and journalists for the first time.

Rising Tensions

Pol Pot knew that numerous Vietnamese troops remained in the country near the border of Cambodia. Many were soldiers who had never left following the pullout at the end of the Second Indochina War. To Pol Pot, these troops posed an enormous security risk and a potential for future aggression. From 1975 onward, the relationship between the countries grew increasingly tense as Pol Pot's troops continued to execute small invasions and confront Vietnamese troops.

As relations deteriorated between the countries, Pol Pot arranged for China to provide aid and troops should full-scale war break out with Vietnam. However, the Chinese were unhappy that Pol Pot and his party were hiding their Communist affiliation from the world. Despite Pol Pot's desire for secrecy and anonymity, in September 1977, at China's insistence, Pol Pot recorded a five-hour speech for Radio Phnom Penh in which he revealed the existence of the CPK/Khmer

Tiananmen Square. This was the first time he had come out into the open since he had fled Phnom Penh fourteen years earlier, and photographs taken during this visit allowed him to be identified by intelligence organizations for the first time as Saloth Sar.

From China, Pol Pot went to Communist North Korea, where he received accolades from government leaders and where the first biographical information about him was broadcast on radio. The fictitious portrait described him as a rubber plant worker who had been brought up on his parents' farm. It also said that he had developed his political ideologies prior to World War II rather than during the early 1950s. Although it mentioned his years in Paris, the portrait inflated his importance to the radical student group, portraying him as the organizer and leader.

Deterioration

When Pol Pot returned from his trip to China and North Korea, the military conflict with Vietnam had escalated. Aggression on the part of Democratic Kampuchea had increased throughout the first half of 1977, including numerous attacks on Vietnamese villages where unarmed civilians were frequently massacred. Additionally, within Cambodia's borders, the few Vietnamese left in the country—many of them women married to Khmer men—were hunted down and killed by the CPK/Khmer Rouge or imprisoned in S-21, where they were abused and then killed.

CPK/Khmer Rouge fighters receive medical treatment after engaging Vietnamese forces.

Rouge and outlined the party's philosophies.

The speech was played on the day he arrived in China for a state visit. There he was treated with great importance and was given a hero's welcome by more than one hundred thousand people in Beijing's

Just prior to Pol Pot's return, the Vietnamese had launched a large, successful retaliatory raid into Cambodia. The Vietnamese attacked and then retreated, taking with them hundreds of prisoners. Pol Pot ordered massive attacks on Vietnamese villages. The aggression by Cambodia seemed like insanity to many who understood that Vietnamese troops far outranked the Cambodians in training and in weapons. However, Pol Pot believed that the Vietnamese had been weakened by the Second Indochina War and that he would receive troops from China. He

was in error; although China provided weapons and money, the haphazardly trained CPK/Khmer Rouge was forced to fight alone.

The military conflicts increased hardship inside the country. People were still expected to maintain impossible quotas of agricultural production. Leaders of districts that failed to do so risked execution, so reports were falsified to show that rice production was meeting quotas. Rice needed to supply communes within districts was sent to the capital as surplus that was exchanged with China for weapons or sent

Cambodian refugees seek shelter at a camp on the Thai border. Cambodia's conflict with Vietnam left many people homeless.

to soldiers on the border. One CPK/
Khmer Rouge member recalled:

> The people did not have enough to
> eat or to wear, and were worked to
> death. At the same time . . . the
> upper levels did not investigate the
> . . . situation but simply sat in their
> offices reading reports and believing
> them. Meanwhile at the lower level,
> the cadres were [trying] to please
> [Angkar] and hiding facts from it. [44]

Culture of Fear

Many within the country began to doubt
the leadership, but only in secret. Spies
were abundant, particularly among children, who were favored for being less corrupted and therefore more trustworthy.
The children frequently spied on people
and turned in even their family members.
One villager recalled:

> They used to tell us that Angkar has
> eyes everywhere like a pineapple.
> Even in the cooperatives, if you felt
> like speaking up you did not dare
> because if they had the slightest sus-
> picion that you might be resistant to
> the disciplines of Angkar they'd take
> you straight off and kill you. The
> spies were even people from our vil-
> lage. They were ordered to do every-
> thing that Angkar commanded. . . .
> For the most part they would be
> young children about 12 years old.
> These children would be so indoc-

trinated that they'd even consider
their own parents enemies. [45]

By 1977, the number of Khmer deaths
in the country resulting from Pol Pot's
policies numbered an estimated 1.2 million. The U.S. State Department reported flagrant and systematic violation of
human rights by the government, including the massive relocation of urban pop-
ulations and brutality against political
opponents.

Indeed, the persecution of perceived
enemies intensified in 1977–1978 as Pol
Pot prepared the country for war. He
came to believe that more and more of his
own CPK/Khmer Rouge members were
hatching plots against him. Further, when
military defeats occurred, officers and
troops were frequently rounded up and
evacuated from the border regions to the
stricter northwestern zones. After a defeat
in 1977 when the Vietnamese had taken
thousands of prisoners back across the
border, including civilians who went voluntarily to seek sanctuary, tens of thousands of CPK/Khmer Rouge soldiers
were evacuated to the northwest, accused
of having Vietnamese minds—that is,
being more loyal to Vietnam. During the
evacuation, thousands of the troops were
massacred.

By January 1978 approximately sixty
thousand Vietnamese troops were in
Cambodia, ready to strike. Despite more
than one offer of peace negotiations from
the Vietnamese, Pol Pot was determined
and optimistic. He was also cavalier about

Khmer youth pose with automatic weapons. Pol Pot recruited and trained a number of children as spies to betray anyone who was disloyal to his regime.

the human toll the war was taking on his own people. He said, "We are not worried that the source of our army would become exhausted, for the people of the lower classes are very numerous."[46]

Pol Pot Opens the Doors

Despite his optimism, however, Pol Pot felt that he needed to make some alliances with countries besides China for aid and support. However, since Cambodia had been isolated from most of the world since the revolution, this required Pol Pot to ease security restrictions and to disguise the hardship imposed by his government

so that other countries would be sympathetic and support the Cambodian struggle against the Vietnamese, whom Pol Pot portrayed as invaders.

Pol Pot made some superficial changes in policy to improve the standard of living of many Cambodians. Among the changes were allowances for time off from work and the reopening of some primary schools. Additionally, in certain zones, he allowed individuals to begin wearing colorful clothing. He announced plans to reintroduce money and a mixed economy in 1979, and he declared amnesty against the "new people," although it was not clear

Enemies Within

In December 1976, during a meeting of members of the Democratic Kampuchean government, the leadership discussed achievements and difficulties from the past year. Reprinted in a collection of documents from the Pol Pot regime, Pol Pot Plans the Future: Confidential Leadership Documents from Democratic Kampuchea, 1976–77, *is a document attributed to Pol Pot that includes a passage dealing with "enemies from within." In the passage, he discusses concerns of traitors within the CPK and DK government. These concerns led to wide-scale purges within the regime.*

A group of traitors has hidden and buried itself inside our flesh and blood. They have big plans. They would destroy our leadership; they would dissolve the Kampuchean revolution. They would take Kampuchea and make it dependent on foreign policies. We have driven them out by means of our beautiful socialist revolution, thus safeguarding our lofty revolution, and on the basis of our accurate policies.

From this experience, we can see that key factors in expelling these enemies have been the leadership of the Party. . . .

Enemies from without continue to approach; enemies within our frontiers haven't yet been eliminated. . . . Enemies concealed within our ranks have not been eliminated either. . . . [T]hose who were hidden before are waking up and haven't been expelled. The old ones who remain in place give birth to new ones, one or two at a time, or so it goes. . . .

The big problem is in the interior. Whether the enemies succeed or not, this remains a serious problem for us. We must resist spies along the frontier, but the important thing is to guard against them in the interior of the country. If we have this kind of policy, no enemy can do anything to us.

how this measure would improve their lives. Despite these improvements, the secret purges and executions persisted. S-21 remained busy, admitting several thousand new prisoners in 1977 and 1978. Further, the regime's eight-point policy was still enforced: Religion, family relations, and unapproved marriages were still forbidden, and collective labor and communal living persisted.

Pol Pot also improved the conditions of Cambodians returning from foreign countries. Since the revolution, citizens sympathetic to the revolution had returned from the United States, Europe, and elsewhere to participate in the new society. However, because they may have been influenced and corrupted by imperialism while they were abroad, many were immediately executed upon arrival. Others were sent to the harshest labor camps or sent to work in factories. In order to improve appearances and to bring more volunteers into the armed forces, these expatriated Cambodians were given better treatment. They were sent to schools where they were indoctrinated with the party's dogma, and a number of the better-educated expatriates were allowed to set up a university under the guidance of Thiounn Mumm.

Once the changes were in place, Pol Pot admitted carefully selected journalists and politicians from various countries into Cambodia. Pro-Communist delegations from Asia, Eastern and Western Europe,

and the United States were allowed in. Pol Pot also gave his first televised interview to a Yugoslavian journalist in which he gave an account of his life. However, he concealed his name, his privileged education, and his background.

Celebrity

The Yugoslavian interview was broadcast on French television. Several people recognized Pol Pot as Saloth Sar, including former associate Keng Vannsak and one of his former high school students.

Pol Pot also increasingly came out into the open within Cambodia. For the first time he was given some of the acclaim

CPK/Khmer Rouge soldiers execute a prisoner in a field. As Pol Pot grew increasingly paranoid, he executed supposed dissidents in greater numbers.

that had surrounded leaders such as Stalin and Mao. References to government policies increasingly noted his name rather than just Angkar. He came to be referred to as Uncle Brother and Brother Number One, and large photographs were hung in communal dining halls. One afternoon in 1978, a poster of Pol Pot went up in a dining hall in Kompong Cham; his image was immediately recognized by Loth Suong, Saloth's brother, who, like other Cambodians, had been forced into collective labor. It was only then that Loth realized that it was his younger brother who had been running the country. Terrified, Loth kept quiet.

Aside from these small propaganda efforts, Pol Pot's publicity efforts were limited because of his paranoia and obsession over security. He still maintained a low profile as much as possible and kept himself and his leaders under tight security, rarely exposing himself to situations where he might be assassinated, such as speaking before large crowds, which Mao and Stalin had regularly done to stir morale.

Plans for the Future

When Pol Pot did speak publicly, it was to small groups of party members, such as the national congress of CPK/Khmer Rouge leaders, which convened in Sept-

Anticelebrities

In Brother Number One: A Political Biography of Pol Pot, *David P. Chandler discusses the reasons for and consequences of Pol Pot and Nuon Chea's preference for maintaining a low profile during their time in power.*

Except for Nuon Chea, Pol Pot was the least accessible Cambodian leader since World War II. Given the extent of the two men's power between 1975 and 1979, we must assume that their inaccessibility was deliberate. Being hidden provided security and room to maneuver. In a sense they both spent their lives as secret agents, even when they were in charge of seven million people. Their concealment kept their enemies off-balance and convinced their followers and friends that they were working full-time for the revolution. This was probably true, especially since the essence of the revolution ... was keeping themselves in power. Their self-effacement, however, had different effects. Pol Pot's was a key element in the loyalty and affection he commanded from those who managed to get close to him at various points in his career. Many Cambodians who came into his presence found him charismatic, because he embodied the ideals of conduct—self control, elegance, kindheartedness. .... Foreigners brought up to admire ... individuals as "personalities" found him exasperating, hypocritical, and elusive.

ember 1978. There Pol Pot outlined a four-year plan to strengthen Democratic Kampuchea and to defeat the Vietnamese. He outlined a model for the improvement of the agricultural communes across the country, which he wanted to become completely self-sufficient. He said that he wanted the country to take a great leap forward into the status of a developed, industrial country. Further, he warned of the dangers of straying from hard-line Communist economics: "If we open the door to capitalism, we will lose our country." [47]

Pol Pot spoke optimistically about the conflict with Vietnam. He said that Cambodian victory was inevitable; however, as with his plan for the development of the country, his plan to beat Vietnam was without basis in any facts. Rather, he seemed to believe that his goals could be accomplished by sheer will because of the righteousness of Cambodia's cause.

End of the Road

Pol Pot's optimism was strong but misguided. Although China provided aid and armaments, CPK/Khmer Rouge troops were inept and poorly trained, often injuring or killing themselves in accidents with weapons and equipment.

Vietnamese advancements increased in late 1978; then, on December 25, the Vietnamese launched a full-scale invasion with more than one hundred thousand Vietnamese troops and twenty thousand former Khmer troops dedicated to Pol Pot's overthrow. The CPK/Khmer Rouge were outnumbered and outgunned, and, as David Chandler writes, "the country cracked like an egg." [48] The Vietnamese forces overran the country and many CPK/Khmer Rouge voluntarily gave themselves up. As Craig Etcheson observes, "Indeed, many Khmer Rouge welcomed the Vietnamese to put an end to the nightmare the revolution had become." [49]

On January 2, 1979, the ground invasion was supported by a Vietnamese air strike, executed using Soviet aircraft as well as U.S. aircraft captured by the Vietnamese during the Second Indochina War.

By January 5, Pol Pot was holed up in Phnom Penh. For the first time since 1973, he met with Sihanouk. Sihanouk later recalled their two-hour meeting as very pleasant. Pol Pot spoke deferentially to Sihanouk, using the formal terms of respect that any of the prince's subjects would. Sihanouk characterized Pol Pot as "a perfect host" and "really very charming." [50] According to Sihanouk, Pol Pot still remained certain of victory over the Vietnamese even as they pressed in toward the capital.

On January 7, 1979, Phnom Penh fell to the Vietnamese. Pol Pot and his top leaders were evacuated by helicopter to Thailand, where they were given asylum in the city of Trat, near the western border of Cambodia. Three days later, the Vietnamese installed a satellite government in Phnom Penh headed by former Democratic Kampuchea officers who had fled during the height of the purges in

Khmer soldiers take cover as they wait for a Vietnamese attack. On Christmas Day, 1978, the Vietnamese launched a full-scale invasion of Cambodia.

1977–1978, as well as by Khmer Communists who had fled in the 1950s. The government, called the People's Republic of Kampuchea (PRK), had as its main aim to prevent Pol Pot's regime from returning to power.

During the less than four years of Pol Pot's regime, between 1.5 and 3 million Khmer died because of his inept and brutal policies and actions. However, Pol Pot remained certain that his government was virtuous and destined to rule, and he was far from ready to give up. For almost two more decades, he would fight to reestablish himself and the CPK/Khmer Rouge in power.

Chapter Seven

Leader in Exile

Having fled to the Thai border after the fall of Democratic Kampuchea in 1979, Pol Pot spent the next nineteen years living in exile in camps on both sides of the northern and eastern Cambodian border, protected by what remained of the CPK/Khmer Rouge who still held territory inside Cambodia near the border regions.

The Thai, along with Chinese and Western powers—particularly the United States—provided financial, tactical, and diplomatic support for him and his exiled regime for much of the 1980s and 1990s. During this time, Pol Pot continued to train and indoctrinate soldiers, order assaults on the Cambodian government, and prepare the CPK/Khmer Rouge for what he believed was their certain return to power.

Unexpected Friends

Despite the unpopularity and hardship of the CPK/Khmer Rouge government, most Khmer feared the Vietnamese and thus hundreds of thousands of Cambodians fled the country toward Thailand to escape the Vietnamese invasion in 1979. Many thousands of refugees were killed in combat or died of disease and starvation on their way; however, those who survived were housed by the Thai in refugee camps along the border, guarded and ruled by CPK/Khmer Rouge soldiers.

Pol Pot and his officers also sought refuge in Thailand, in a camp code-named Office 87 near the village of Trat just a few miles inside the Thai border. While relations between Pol Pot's government and the Thai had been difficult during the regime's rule, the Thai were willing to

After the Vietnamese took control of Cambodia, Pol Pot fled to Thailand.

saw Vietnam as an increasing threat. Likewise, China feared the rising power of a state supported by the Soviet Union because, since the mid-1960s, China and Russia had become rivals for dominance as the strongest Communist world power. Therefore, China offered its support.

Additionally, the United States began immediate financial support to Pol Pot and the CPK/Khmer Rouge. The Americans were an unexpected ally for the Cambodian Communists; the U.S. government saw the Vietnamese Communist government as an enemy and, like Pol Pot's regime, had an interest in damaging the PRK.

Discovery of Horrors

The new PRK government was openly pro-Vietnamese. A month after the fall of the DK, the PRK and the Socialist Republic of Vietnam signed a twenty-five-year friendship treaty, which both China and the CPK/Khmer Rouge immediately denounced. The PRK also attacked the Pol Pot regime, making public its discovery of many of the remnants of its brutal policies. They uncovered the mass graves in the Killing Fields around the country as well as at S-21. In the last days of the Vietnamese assault, the CPK/Khmer Rouge had executed many prisoners, and their dead bodies remained at S-21. Of the many thousands who had been imprisoned there, fewer than ten survived to tell what they and others had suffered. The Vietnamese also discovered documentation, including photos of each

protect Pol Pot and the CPK/Khmer Rouge because they proved to be useful allies against the Vietnamese. For many years, Cambodia had served as a physical buffer between Thailand and Vietnam, and after the fall of DK, the Thai prisoner processed at the prison, attesting to the scope of the killings that had taken place there.

In the meantime, the PRK immediately began dismantling the oppressive policies of the Pol Pot regime. Markets, schools, and hospitals were reopened. Freedom of movement, association, and practice of religion was again permitted. Families could reunite and again live, eat, and farm together, and money was reintroduced.

Trial of Absent Despots

Among the first official acts the PRK took against the Pol Pot regime was to put Pol Pot and Ieng Sary on trial in August 1979 for crimes of genocide. Court documents charged that

[the] Pol Pot–Ieng Sary clique . . . planned massacres of groups of innocent people; expulsion of inhabitants of cities and villages in order to concentrate them and force them to do

Pictured is one of the metal bed frames to which inmates of S-21 were bound during torture. Only seven prisoners survived to tell of the camp's horrors.

hard labor in conditions leading to their physical and mental destruction; wiping out religion; destroying political, cultural, and social structures and family social relations. [51]

Since the two men were in hiding, they were tried in absentia, which was allowed by international law when defendants refuse to appear. Pol Pot and Ieng Sary were notified of the trial through the media, but they did not show up. Pol and Ieng were provided a defense of three attorneys—two Cambodians and one American who, since they could not contact the defendants, made arguments of their own invention.

During the trial, hundreds of witnesses came forward to give accounts of the abuses suffered under the Pol Pot regime. Emotions in the courtroom ran high as many in the audience wept through the testimony. Upon hearing the testimony, one witness to the proceedings concluded that "the methods used by Pol Pot, Ieng Sary, and their associates, which could get rid of hundreds of thousands of people at a time, were far crueler than those adopted by Hitler." [52]

Both of the defendants were found guilty and sentenced to death, a punishment to be carried out if they were ever captured. This sentence remained in effect but unexecuted against Ieng Sary until he

The bones and skulls of victims of S-21 are arranged in the geographical shape of Cambodia as part of a museum display in Phnom Penh.

gave himself up and against Pol Pot until his death. Although the sentences were never carried out, the trial itself was significant because it was the first exercise of antigenocide laws established following the Nazi Holocaust of World War II and because it set a precedent for future genocide trials in Bosnia and Rwanda.

In an interview given in the early 1980s, Pol Pot, although he admitted some error in the DK administration, was unrepentant and denied the crimes for which he had been convicted. When asked about the killings in his country, he said, "Only several thousand Kampucheans might have died due to some mistake in implementing our policy of providing an affluent life for the people." Further, he compared the actions of Vietnam to those of Hitler and claimed that his regime was being blamed for Vietnam's crimes: "Hitler killed the Jews and those who opposed him. Vietnam kills those who oppose it and innocent people who will not join it."[53]

The New Armed Struggle

From his camp in northern Cambodia, Pol Pot—along with his associates Ieng Sary, Khieu Samphan, Son Sen, and others—continued to control the CPK/Khmer Rouge. Although he officially resigned from the position of prime minister in 1982 and turned the job over to Khieu Samphan, he still maintained the number-one position of power. The decision to step down was a strategy to downplay his visibility because his extremism was getting bad press. In fact,

Three Cambodian boys stand in front of a hut containing the remains of some of the victims of Pol Pot's campaign of genocide.

after 1982, Pol Pot did not grant an interview for more than ten years, even refusing an offer of $3 million from a U.S. television network. Thus Khieu became the public face of the DK government in exile, while Pol Pot remained behind the scenes, teaching and training. CPK/Khmer Rouge officers were sent to Office 87 for intensive thirteen-day sessions with the leaders to receive indoctrination.

Further, the CPK/Khmer Rouge received secret military aid, arms, and training from various countries. Arms were supplied directly and indirectly by China, France, Sweden, Singapore, West Germany, the United States, and Great Britain.

Throughout the 1980s, the most significant patrons of Pol Pot were China, the United States, and Great Britain. Between the years 1980 and 1986, the U.S. government supplied Pol Pot's regime with over $85 million in aid. Further, the United States pressured the international World Food Program to send $12 million to the Thai army, which passed the food along to the CPK/Khmer Rouge.

Secretly, the CIA, along with Britain's Special Air Service and MI6 (its intelligence agency), supplied the CPK/Khmer Rouge with training in military strategy, guerrilla tactics, weapons handling, and mine placing. This last tactic was particularly damaging to the safety of Cambodian civilians. The CPK/Khmer Rouge laid thousands of mines throughout the country in the 1980s and early 1990s. These mines caused death or grievous injuries to many thousands of people. The injuries also caused even greater economic crises because farmers lost limbs and were consequently unable to work their land. By the early 1990s, eighty patients a week were being admitted and treated in ill-equipped hospitals, making Cambodia the most disabled nation on Earth.

While the CPK/Khmer Rouge received aid, the Cambodian people suffered. Because the PRK was not recognized by the United Nations (UN), it received no health or humanitarian aid from the world community. Cambodians were deprived of clean water, health assistance, and medicine. Further, to punish the Vietnamese through their satellite government, the United States and China led a trade embargo against Cambodia. In 1989 the United States prevented a UN development aid mission from entering the country, a policy that Pol Pot applauded as "very correct."[54]

Not everyone in the U.S. government was pleased by these actions. In 1990 Massachusetts congressman Chester Atkins said that in its attempt to punish Vietnam, the United States risked returning Pol Pot to power:

> If our assistance overt and covert [is] successful, it will have the direct result of returning the Khmer Rouge to power. . . . I think we're playing a very dangerous game . . . [because] a small group in the State Department and Security Council are still fighting the Vietnam War.[55]

Pol Pot in Exile

Very little of Pol Pot's actions during the 1980s are known. From 1981 to 1986 he virtually disappeared. No photographs, interviews, or accounts are available. There were reports that he had suffered some illness during these years and was taken to Bangkok or Beijing for hospitalization. The first personal details emerged in 1987, when he married for a second time. Since the 1960s his wife Saloth Ponnary, had suffered bouts of mental illness. Despite the fact that the couple still loved each other, they lived apart in separate quarters while she was cared for by a female CPK/Khmer Rouge member. Ponnary had served in an important role in the Democratic Kampuchean government as president of women. However, her health continued to deteriorate in the 1980s. The couple had had no children together.

In 1987, after receiving permission from Ponnary, Pol Pot married a young Cambodian peasant woman, Mea Son. Within a year, she gave birth to a daughter, which Pol Pot gave his own prerevolutionary name, Sar, meaning "white." Pol Pot and his new family lived with him in his compound, and he frequently took his daughter along to training sessions, where she would sit on his lap while he spoke.

A Possible Return to Power

For ten years after the Vietnamese satellite government took power, Pol Pot and the CPK/Khmer Rouge harassed the PRK government with guerrilla raids, sabotage, and other military actions. By 1989, worn down by these actions, the Vietnamese withdrew from Cambodia, leaving the country open for a takeover. Many feared Pol Pot would return to power.

After Pol Pot's regime was toppled, medical services once again became available. Here, victims of the CPK/Khmer Rouge learn to walk with artificial limbs.

The UN Security Council began negotiations to establish a new coalition government, which would represent the main political forces in the country. China insisted that the CPK/Khmer Rouge be installed as part of a coalition government, and in August 1990 the rest of the Security Council agreed to China's demand. In October 1991 a peace agreement was signed by coalition members, including Pol Pot's regime; however, Pol

Pol Pot poses with his daughter in his home in Thailand in 1986.

Pot was determined to take back full power over the country and reneged on the agreement. He refused to let the CPK/Khmer Rouge participate in the 1993 elections, the first free elections held in twenty-three years.

Installed were Sihanouk's son, Prince Norodom Ranariddh, and Hun Sen, a defected CPK/Khmer Rouge member, as co–prime ministers. Sihanouk was reinstalled as chief of state and king of Cambodia, returning to the throne after thirty-eight years. Within the year, the new government outlawed the CPK/Khmer Rouge and began closing in on Pol Pot and his party members. Pol Pot retreated to northern Cambodia, which was still controlled by the CPK/Khmer Rouge. He lived near the village of Anlong Veng in a large, comfortable house with his family, surrounded by his top officers. From there, he continued to plan the overthrow of the government.

Defections

In the mid-1990s, the CPK/Khmer Rouge began to decline. During the 1980s and early 1990s, the CPK/Khmer Rouge had been wealthy, thriving on the profits from foreign aid as well as illegal trade in timber and gems from territory under their control. As international aid dried up and the government closed in, they lost much of their resources. Ammunition, supplies, and food began drying up.

In August 1996 the first mass defections occurred when Ieng Sary, also

Health Concerns

Since the mid-1960s, Pol Pot reportedly suffered from periodic bouts of illness. In 1966 he contracted malaria while on his way north to Vietnam, a disease that troubled him for the remainder of his life. Throughout his time in power, he succumbed to periodic bouts of the disease as well as to intestinal disorders. The first such recurrence of malaria was in September 1976. Pol Pol temporarily resigned as prime minister, and Nuon Chea acted in his place. Many speculate that the resignation was possibly a tactic to confuse his enemies within the party, to encourage them to show themselves in his absence so that he could crush them once he returned to power.

During the 1980s and 1990s, rumors about Pol Pot's health surfaced regularly. Many suggested he was terminally ill. It is known that he was frequently hospitalized in Bangkok and Beijing, but the nature of the illnesses is not known. Finally, in interviews given before his death, Pol Pot expressed general concerns about his health. Many attribute his death in 1998 to these health concerns; others are skeptical, maintaining that he was murdered or committed suicide.

known as Brother Number Three, became the first senior leader of the CPK/Khmer Rouge to turn himself in. Because Ieng had given himself up voluntarily, the government made an example of him to encourage others to leave the CPK/Khmer Rouge. Instead of being prosecuted, Ieng was granted a royal pardon and given a luxurious villa in Phnom Penh. He was also given control of the eastern village of Pailin to rule as his own fiefdom, where he created a refuge for other CPK/Khmer Rouge, including his wife, Ieng Thirith, and Pol Pot's first wife, Saloth Ponnary, who went to live with them.

After Ieng's defection, battalions of CPK/Khmer Rouge began surrendering one by one. The government announced that it would give amnesty to defectors, and as soldiers turned themselves in, they were given new coalition government uniforms and sent to fight against their old leaders.

In 1997 nearly half the CPK/Khmer Rouge forces broke from Pol Pot's regime and made a deal with the Cambodian government. In June King Sihanouk announced he would consider granting amnesty to senior officers Khieu Samphan, Son Sen, and Nuon Chea; however, he said that he would never grant amnesty to Pol Pot or to Ta Mok, the CPK/Khmer Rouge military chief.

That month, Pol Pot retaliated against the defections. He executed his top aide, Son Sen, whom he held responsible for the mass desertions, and had his family brutally murdered. Fearing for his own safety, Ta Mok arrested Pol Pot and placed him on trial in a secret location in the jungle outside Anlong Veng.

Trial of Pol Pot

On June 25, 1997, Ta Mok and the other CPK/Khmer Rouge leaders placed Pol Pot on trial for treason. They accused him of preventing the CPK/Khmer Rouge from participating in the coalition government and of the murder of Son Sen and his family.

A U.S. journalist, Nate Thayer, was brought in by the CPK/Khmer Rouge to

In addition to Pol Pot, the CPK/Khmer Rouge leadership included (clockwise from bottom left) Ta Mok, Khieu Samphan, Nuon Chea, and Ieng Sary.

witness the trial, in which Pol Pot was found guilty. He reported that the denunciation of Pol Pot seemed genuine: "There was a debate within the leadership on whether to, in fact, kill [Pol Pot], cut him off from medical care and allow him to live his final days under house detention." [56] The decision was made to sentence him to life imprisonment under house arrest. Many denounced the proceedings as a show trial, meant not to dispense justice but to win political sympathy for the CPK/Khmer Rouge. As legal analyst Steven Ratner observed:

> What [the trial was] was something reminiscent of the show trials that Stalin put on in the 30s and took place in China during the Cultural Revolution. It's not real justice. . . . I would also underline the fact that it is very much focusing on one person when, in fact, [the regime] was a movement with many people, most of whom are beyond . . . the scope of justice at this point. [57]

End of Pol Pot

Despite the trial and the denunciation, Pol Pot denied the extent of the atrocities under his leadership, including the existence of S-21. He remained unrepentant, continuing to blame the Vietnamese for the violence, saying that everything he did was necessary to defend himself from them. In 1997, in the first interview given since the early 1980s, Pol Pot said, "I came

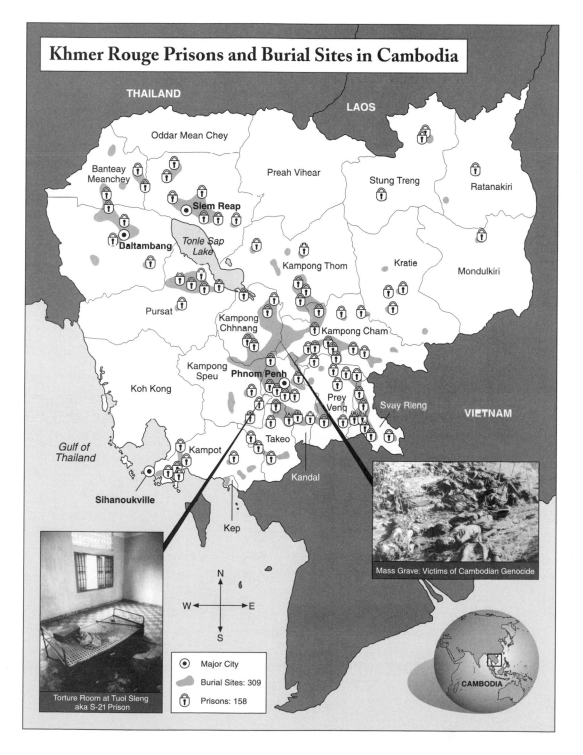

Khmer Rouge Prisons and Burial Sites in Cambodia

THAILAND

LAOS

Oddar Mean Chey

Banteay
Meanchey

Preah Vihear

Stung Treng

Ratanakiri

Siem Reap

Daltambang

Tonle Sap
Lake

Kampong Thom

Kratie

Mondulkiri

Pursat

Kampong
Chhnang

Kampong Cham

Kampong
Speu

Phnom Penh

Koh Kong

Prey
Veng

Svay Rieng

VIETNAM

Gulf of
Thailand

Kampot

Takeo

Kandal

Sihanoukville

Kep

Mass Grave: Victims of Cambodian Genocide

N
W   E
S

Torture Room at Tuol Sleng
aka S-21 Prison

⊙   Major City

      Burial Sites: 309

      Prisons: 158

CAMBODIA

Cheating Justice

Reactions to Pol Pot's death came from all over the world. They were predominantly expressions of relief that he could not return to power. Many others expressed anger and disappointment that Pol Pot had escaped justice. Several of the reactions quoted here are from the collection by the Cambodian Institute for Cooperation and Peace titled Skepticism, Outrage, Hope: Reactions to the Death of Pol Pot.

"Pol Pot's death left me angry because he died better than the average Khmer people. He died clothed like a normal Khmer citizen instead of his revolutionary communist outfit. He died too comfortably resting on a mattress bed where such a luxury is beyond the dream of his own Khmer people or even average Khmer citizens. . . . [H]e does not deserve such a dignified death."

—Kenneth T. So

"I suffered. My father, my brother, and my brother-in-law were killed during Pol Pot's regime. If Pol Pot is really dead he will be judged in hell. If he is really dead, I'm very sorry because the international community is too late to bring him to justice. They should not have delayed in arresting Pol Pot from 1979 to now. How can we find justice now for those . . . who died during his rule?" —Chey Sopheara, director of the Toul Sleng Museum (former site of S-21)

"Pol Pot was the answer to the question, there can never be another Hitler. In the full view of the world, he created his own holocaust and yet no government would intervene to stop the bloodshed. Anytime Pol Pot's name is mentioned, people have horrific thoughts. Also, we are reminded of our own impotence." —Allan Goodman, Georgetown University's Foreign Service School

to carry out the struggle, not to kill people. Even now, and you can look at me, am I a savage person?"[58]

Although he protested his innocence, the CPK/Khmer Rouge rapidly evaporated around him. In 1998 Nuon Chea and Khieu Samphan defected and were granted pardons by the Cambodian government. They joined Ieng Sary in his haven in Pailin. Behind them, hundreds more troops continued to defect. Additionally, former CPK/Khmer Rouge members eventually entered the coalition government.

In March 1998 Cambodian forces attacked Anlong Veng to capture the remaining CPK/Khmer Rouge leaders. Ta Mok fled into the jungle with Pol Pot as his prisoner. There Pol Pot was held with his wife in a two-room hut only a few hundred yards from the Thai border.

On April 15, 1998, Pol Pot reportedly heard on the radio that Ta Mok planned to turn him over to the U.S. government, which, under international pressure, had been calling for his arrest and trial before an international court for the crime of genocide. That evening, he told his wife that he did not feel well and went to lie down. At 10:00 P.M. he was found dead in his bed. The CPK/Khmer Rouge reported that he had died of a heart attack, but two days later, before an autopsy could be performed, his body was cremated without ceremony on a pile of old tires and mattresses in a clearing near his hut. The fact that the body was cremated before being examined led many to believe that Pol Pot either committed suicide or was murdered. Whatever the cause of his death, Pol Pot's final resting place is a garbage dump in the middle of the jungle.

Legacy of Terror and Hatred

Few mourned the death of Pol Pot, and many within Cambodia were greatly relieved, finally certain that he could never return to power. Yet the nightmarish policies of the Pol Pot regime left Cambodia permanently scarred. Decades later, few lives in the country are without link to someone who died at the hands of the CPK/Khmer Rouge or who committed atrocities under their orders. Further, despite government efforts to eradicate the thousands of land mines laid by the CPK/Khmer Rouge, people are still maimed and killed. As recently as 2003, nine hundred people were injured or killed by mines.

The body of Pol Pot lies in his Thailand home in 1998. Many Cambodians were outraged that Pol Pot was not brought to justice before he died.

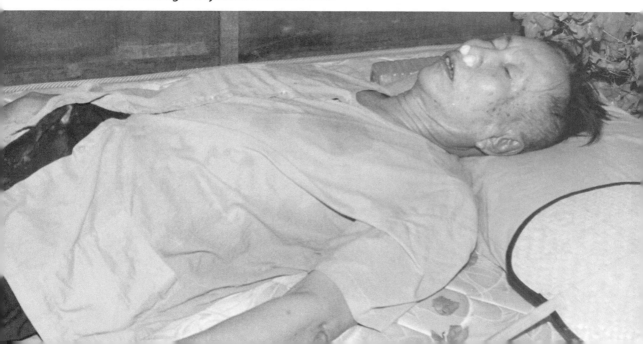

Many who lived through the Pol Pot regime strive to remind and teach Cambodians about the period so that it might not be repeated. For example, the Sleng Genocide Museum, now housed on the former S-21 prison, remains as a reminder of the torture and abuse perpetrated by the Santebal under Pol Pot.

In contrast, near Anlong Veng, where some villagers remain loyal, the local government sponsored a CPK/Khmer Rouge theme park in 2004. It includes sites such as Pol Pot's luxurious house, complete with underground concrete bunker and swimming pool and his gravesite. Many critics have objected. According to Youk Chang of the Documentation Centre of Cambodia, which is charged with collecting documentation and testimonies about CPK/Khmer Rouge atrocities: "Buying a ticket to see the grave of Pol Pot undermines the value of the memories and the suffering we've been through."[59]

Although supporters of Pol Pot and the CPK/Khmer Rouge do remain, Pol Pot ranks among the most notorious villains in Cambodia and around the world. He penetrated the minds of Cambodians so deeply that even today he is spoken of like a supernatural monster or bogeyman. However, as David Etcheson points out, this conception belies the truth:

> Some people think that he must be an evil god or a monster or some kind of inhuman creature, but in fact these kinds of things are not done by monsters, they are not done by gods. Genocides are carried out by human beings, by politicians, and this is what Pol Pot was.[60]

Indeed, to many, the legacy that Pol Pot left behind remains as a testament to the evil of which human beings are capable.

NOTES

Chapter One: A Privileged Youth

1. Ben Kiernan, *The Pol Pot Regime: Race, Power, and Genocide in Cambodia Under the CPK/Khmer Rouge, 1975–79.* New Haven, CT: Yale University Press, 2002, p. 10.
2. Quoted in Ben Kiernan, *How Pol Pot Came to Power.* London: Verso, 1985, p. 27.
3. Quoted in David P. Chandler, *Brother Number One: A Political Biography of Pol Pot.* Boulder, CO: Westview, 1992, p. 9.
4. Quoted in Chandler, *Brother Number One*, p. 17.
5. Quoted in Chandler, *Brother Number One*, p. 19.
6. Quoted in Chandler, *Brother Number One*, p. 20.

Chapter Two: A Political Awakening

7. Quoted in Home Vision Entertainment, *The Red Masters*, vol. 3: *Pol Pot: Man of Genocide*, 2002.
8. Chandler, *Brother Number One*, pp. 29–30.
9. Quoted in Home Vision Entertainment, *Pol Pot: Man of Genocide*.
10. Quoted in Home Vision Entertainment, *Pol Pot: Man of Genocide*.
11. Quoted in Craig Etcheson, *The Rise and Demise of Democratic Kampuchea.* Boulder, CO: Westview, 1984, p. 51.

12. Kiernan, *The Pol Pot Regime*, p. 12.
13. Quoted in Home Vision Entertainment, *Pol Pot: Man of Genocide*.
14. Etcheson, *The Rise and Demise of Democratic Kampuchea*, p. 49.
15. Quoted in Kiernan, *How Pol Pot Came to Power*, p. 122.

Chapter Three: Revolutionary

16. Quoted in Kiernan, *The Pol Pot Regime*, p. 11.
17. Quoted in Chandler, *Brother Number One*, p. 44.
18. Chandler, *Brother Number One*, p. 44.
19. Quoted in Chandler, *Brother Number One*, p. 54.

Chapter Four: Rising to Power

20. David Chandler, "Time 100: Pol Pot," *Time Asia*, August 23–30, 1999. www.time.com/time/asia/asia/magazine/1999/990823/pol_pot1.html.
21. Quoted in Kiernan, *How Pol Pot Came to Power*, p. 220.
22. Etcheson, *The Rise and Demise of Democratic Kampuchea*, p. 147.
23. Chandler, "Time 100: Pol Pot."
24. Quoted in Etcheson, *The Rise and Fall of Democratic Kampuchea*, p. 70.
25. Quoted in Chandler, *Brother Number One*, p. 84.
26. Quoted in Home Vision Entertainment, *Pol Pot: Man of Genocide*.

27. Chandler, *Brother Number One*, p. 104.

Chapter Five: Ruler in the Shadows

28. Edward S. Herman, "Pol Pot's Death in the Propaganda System," *Z Magazine*, June 1998, p. 12.
29. Etcheson, *The Rise and Fall of Democratic Kampuchea*, p. 144.
30. Quoted in Kiernan, *The Pol Pot Regime*, p. 54.
31. Quoted in James Pringle, "Surviving in the Land That Justice Forgot," *Sunday Tribune* (Ireland), February 16, 2003, p. 23.
32. Quoted in Home Vision Entertainment, *Pol Pot: Man of Genocide*.
33. Kiernan, *The Pol Pot Regime*, pp. 8–9.
34. Quoted in Chandler, *Brother Number One*, p. 110.
35. Quoted in Chandler, "Time 100: Pol Pot."
36. Quoted in Home Vision Entertainment, *Pol Pot: Man of Genocide*.
37. Quoted in Chandler, *Brother Number One*, p. 105.
38. Quoted in Kiernan, *The Pol Pot Regime*, p. 3
39. David Chandler, *Voices from S-21: Terror and History in Pol Pot's Secret Prison*. Berkeley and Los Angeles: University of California Press, 1999, p. 7.
40. Quoted in INA and ARTE France, *S21, the Khmer Rouge Killing Machine*. Brooklyn, NY: First Run/Icarus Films, 2002.
41. Quoted in Martin Regg Cohn, "In the Forgotten Killing Fields," *Toronto Star*, January 26, 2003, p. B05.

42. Quoted in Chandler, *Brother Number One*, p. 136.
43. Quoted in Home Vision Entertainment, *Pol Pot: Man of Genocide*.

Chapter Six: Brother Number One

44. Quoted in David P. Chandler, *The Tragedy of Cambodian History: Politics, War, and Revolution Since 1945*. New Haven, CT: Yale University Press, 1991, p. 270.
45. Quoted in Home Vision Entertainment, *Pol Pot: Man of Genocide*.
46. Quoted in Kiernan, *How Pol Pot Came to Power*, p. 428.
47. Quoted in Chandler, *Brother Number One*, p. 167.
48. Chandler, "Time 100: Pol Pot."
49. Quoted in Home Vision Entertainment, *Pol Pot: Man of Genocide*.
50. Quoted in Chandler, *Brother Number One*, p. 164.

Chapter Seven: Leader in Exile

51. Quoted in Howard J. De Nike, John Quigley, and Kenneth J. Robinson, eds., *Genocide in Cambodia: Documents from the Trial of Pol Pot and Ieng Sary*. Philadelphia: University of Pennsylvania Press, 2000, p. 45.
52. Quoted in BBC, "Trial of Pol Pot and Ieng Sary Opens in Phnom Penh," BBC Summary of World Broadcasts, August 17, 1979.
53. Quoted in Chandler, *Brother Number One*, p. 171.
54. Quoted in Central Independent Television, *Cambodia: The Betrayal: A Special*

Report by John Pilger. New York: Filmmakers Library, 1993.

55. Quoted in Central Independent Television, *Cambodia: The Betrayal.*

56. Quoted in Public Broadcasting System, "The People's Verdict," transcript of *PBS Online News Hour:* "Justice for Pol Pot?" August 6, 1997.

57. Quoted in Public Broadcasting System, "The People's Verdict."

58. Quoted in Chandler, "Time 100: Pol Pot."

59. Quoted in Alan Sipress, "Restoring Pol Pot's Hideout," *Gazette* (Montreal), April 25, 2004, p. D5.

60. Quoted in Central Independent Television, *Cambodia: The Betrayal.*

CHRONOLOGY

May 19, 1928
Saloth Sar is born in the village of Prek Sbauv in the Kompong Thom region of Cambodia.

1934
Saloth moves to Phnom Penh to live with his brother, sister, and cousin, and to attend school; he spends two years as a novice studying at a Buddhist monastery.

1936
Saloth attends the private French primary school École Miche in Phnom Penh.

1942
Saloth attends boarding school, Collège Sihanouk, in Kompong Cham.

1945
Japan takes over much of Indochina and imprisons French officials; Cambodia is independent from March to October.

1946
First Indochina War breaks out in Vietnam; Cambodia drafts its first constitution.

1947
Saloth works for the Democrats in preparation for the National Assembly elections; he also meets Ieng Sary.

1948
Saloth fails entrance examination to Lycée Sisowath and enrolls at École technique in Phnom Pehn.

1949
Saloth receives a scholarship to study radio-electricity in France; he arrives in Paris in September.

1950–1952
Saloth is involved with a group of politically radical Khmer intellectuals studying in Paris, writes first published essay attacking the Sihanouk monarchy, and becomes a member of the French Communist Party.

1953
Saloth returns to Phnom Penh after losing his scholarship; he joins a Khmer/Vietminh unit in eastern Cambodia.

1954
Saloth returns to Phnom Penh and works with Democrats to radicalize and unify the opposition parties against Sihanouk in the 1955 election campaign.

1955
Sihanouk's Sangkum Party wins rigged elections, severely damaging the Democratic Party.

1956

Saloth begins teaching in Phnom Penh, marries Khieu Ponnary, and works secretly for the Communists.

1960

Saloth participtes in a secret Cambodian Communist Party congress and becomes the third most powerful officer in the new Workers Party of Kampuchea (WPK).

1962

Saloth takes over as secretary general of the WPK after Tou Sammouth disappears.

1963

Saloth's name appears on a list of men wanted for subversive activity by the Sihanouk government; Saloth goes into hiding in eastern Cambodia.

1964

Saloth spends a year at "Office 100" near the eastern Cambodian border.

1965

Saloth meets with Vietnamese Communist leaders in Hanoi, who discourage the WPK from pursuing a struggle for Cambodian independence against Sihanouk; U.S. combat troops arrive in Vietnam, marking the beginning of the Second Indochina War.

1966

Saloth meets with Mao Tse-tung in Beijing during the Cultural Revolution; Sihanouk suffers a setback in National Assembly elections; Saloth returns to Cambodia, changes the name of the WPK to the Communist Party of Kampuchea (CPK), which was known by outsiders as the Khmer Rouge.

1967

Samlaut uprising in the northwest is brutally suppressed by the Sihanouk government, causing the CPK/Khmer Rouge to plan for armed struggle.

1968

A CPK/Khmer Rouge offensive near Battambang marks the beginning of civil war between the Cambodian government and opposition forces.

1969

U.S. bombing of Cambodia greatly intensifies, creating many refugees and recruits for the CPK/Khmer Rouge.

1970

Sihanouk is overthrown in a coup d'état by Lon Nol; Sihanouk joins CPK/Khmer Rouge forces in United Front government to overthrow Lon Nol regime, encouraging thousands of supporters to join the CPK/Khmer Rouge; U.S. and South Vietnamese forces invade eastern Cambodia.

1973

Heaviest U.S. bombing of Cambodia yet; Sihanouk visits CPK/Khmer Rouge leaders at Angkor Wat.

1975–1978

CPK/Khmer Rouge forces capture Phnom Penh; cities are evacuated; Pol Pot regime policies begin behind anonymity of Angkar; Pol Pot's fictitious biography revealed when he is named prime minister of Democratic Kampuchea (DK); extensive purges occur within the DK government; in China, Pol Pot reveals the existence of the CPK/ Khmer Rouge; photographs allow Pol Pot's real identity to be discovered by intelligence agents; war between DK and Vietnam begins.

1979
The DK government falls to Vietnam; Pol Pot and other CPK/Khmer Rouge leaders flee across the Thai border.

1980s
Pol Pot's CPK/Khmer Rouge and its allies continue opposition to new Vietnamese government, receiving diplomatic support, military funding and training, and human-itarian aid from anti-Vietnam countries, including the United States.

1987
Pol Pot remarries; the couple have a daughter named Sar in 1988.

1996–1998
Mass defections of leaders and troops from the CPK/Khmer Rouge.

1998
Pol Pot arrested and tried by the CPK/ Khmer Rouge in a show trial; Pol Pot is sentenced to life under house arrest; on April 15, Pol Pot dies under suspicious circumstances and is cremated on April 17 before an autopsy can be performed.

FOR FURTHER READING

Books

Raoul M. Jennar, ed., *The Cambodian Constitutions (1953–1993)*. Bangkok, Thailand: White Lotus, 1995. Provides the text of the four Cambodian constitutions promulgated between 1953 and 1993. Includes an appendix describing the succession of the throne from the nineteenth century to the present.

Henry Kamm, *Cambodia: Report from a Stricken Land*. New York: Little, Brown, 1998. This book details Cambodian history from the overthrow of Prince Sihanouk in 1970 to the political upheaval within the coalition government of the late 1990s.

Chris Riley and Douglas Niven, eds., *The Killing Fields*. Santa Fe, NM: Twin Palm, 1996. This volume is a collection of mug shots of S-21 prisoners taken by guards as part of processing inmates. Includes an account by former inmate Vann Nath and a short essay by David Chandler.

David L. Snellgrove, *Khmer Civilization and Angkor*. Bangkok, Thailand: Orchid, 2001. This guide to Cambodia's historic temples and sites includes a brief history of the Khmer civilization through the rise and decline of the Khmer Empire. Includes numerous color pictures of significant temples, statuary, and sites.

Pin Yathay with John Man, *Stay Alive, My Son*. New York: Touchstone, 1987. This memoir, written by a Cambodian professional, details the author's life during the Pol Pot regime.

Video

Goldcrest and International Film Investors present an Enigma Production, *The Killing Fields*, Warner Home Video, 1984. Directed by Roland Joffe and based on a true story, this film portrays the story of U.S. journalist Sydney Schanberg and Cambodian photographer and translator Dith Pran, who risked their lives to cover the events leading up to and following the fall of Phnom Penh to the CPK/Khmer Rouge in 1975.

Web Sites

Cambodia e-Gov Home Page (www. cambodia.gov.kh/unisq11/egov/ english/home.view.html). Presents broad information regarding the Cambodian government.

Cambodian Genocide Project (www.yale.edu/cgp). Provides extensive information on the Cambodian genocide, including maps, searchable databases,

photographs, and links to articles and other resources.

Cambodia Information Center (www.cambodia.org). Offers numerous links to facts, photographs, maps, news, and Cambodian cultural information.

WORKS CONSULTED

Books

David P. Chandler, *Brother Number One: A Political Biography of Pol Pot.* Boulder, CO: Westview, 1992. Details the life of Saloth Sar/Pol Pot from birth to exile in 1992.

———, *A History of Cambodia.* Boulder, CO: Westview, 1983. Provides a detailed political and social history of Cambodia from prehistorical times through the mid-twentieth century as the movement toward independence and revolution flourished.

———, *The Tragedy of Cambodian History: Politics, War, and Revolution Since 1945.* New Haven, CT: Yale University Press, 1991. Offers a detailed political history of Cambodia from the end of World War II through the fall of Democratic Kampuchea. Includes an appendix of testimonies from those who lived through the Pol Pot regime as well as an extensive bibliography.

———, *Voices from S-21: Terror and History in Pol Pot's Secret Prison,* Berkeley and Los Angeles: University of California Press, 1999. Gives detailed history and information about the Democratic Kampuchea prison and security headquarters, S-21. Includes pictures and a map of the compound.

David P. Chandler, Ben Kiernan, and Chanthou Boua, trans. and eds., *Pol Pot Plans the Future: Confidential Leadership Documents from Democratic Kampuchea, 1976–1977.* New Haven, CT: Yale University Southeast Asia Studies, 1988. This volume provides memoranda, speech transcriptions, letters, and other documents created by Pol Pot and the DK government during its reign.

Howard J. De Nike, John Quigley, and Kenneth J. Robinson, eds., *Genocide in Cambodia: Documents from the Trial of Pol Pot and Ieng Sary.* Philadelphia: University of Pennsylvania Press, 2000. Provides in-depth coverage, testimony, and analysis of the 1979 trial of the two leaders by the People's Republic of Kampuchea.

Craig Etcheson, *The Rise and Demise of Democratic Kampuchea.* Boulder, CO: Westview, 1984. Provides a historical analysis of the events leading up to, during, and following the Pol Pot regime's rule. Focuses on the revolutionary agenda of the movement and includes detailed charts and time lines.

Kao Kim Hourn and Tania Theriault, eds., *Skepticism, Outrage, Hope: Reactions to the Death of Pol Pot*. Phnom Penh, Cambodia: Cambodian Institute for Cooperation and Peace, 1998. This volume provides a compilation of articles and quotes offered in response to Pol Pot's death in 1998.

Ben Kiernan, *How Pol Pot Came to Power*. London: Verso, 1985. Discusses and analyzes the historical and political events leading to the rise of Pol Pot's regime through the early 1970s.

————, *The Pol Pot Regime: Race, Power, and Genocide in Cambodia Under the Khmer Rouge, 1975–79*. New Haven, CT: Yale University Press, 2002. Examines the role of racist attitudes and beliefs and how they influenced the genocide of the Pol Pot regime.

Marie Alexandrine Martin, *Cambodia: A Shattered Society*, trans. Mark W. McLeod, Berkeley and Los Angeles: University of California Press, 1989. Martin examines the weaknesses and alliances within the prerevolutionary Cambodian government and contends that they led to the political upheaval of the 1970s.

François Pouchard, *Cambodia: Year Zero*, trans. Nancy Amphoux. New York: Holt, Rinehart and Winston, 1978. In this book Pouchard describes the events immediately following the CPK/Khmer Rouge's taking power in 1975. Includes transcriptions of firsthand accounts by Cambodian civilians about their treatment by CPK/Khmer Rouge forces.

Vann Nath, *A Cambodian Prison Portrait: One Year in the Khmer Rouge's S-21*. Bangkok, Thailand: White Lotus, 1998. A personal account written by one of the few survivors of the Pol Pot regime's S-21 prison, including reproductions of paintings by the author depicting the hardship, torture, and abuse endured by prisoners.

Newspapers, Periodicals, and Government Documents

American Foreign Policy, 1950–1955, Basic Documents, Volumes I and II, Publication 6446, General Foreign Policy Series. Washington DC: U.S. Government Printing Office, 1957.

British Broadcasting Corporation, "President Carter's Recent Statements on World Affairs," BBC Summary of World Broadcasts, January 23, 1979.

————, "Trial of Pol Pot and Ieng Sary Opens in Phnom Penh," BBC Summary of World Broadcasts, August 17, 1979.

————, "USA Denounced over Attitude to Pol Pot Representatives at UN," BBC Summary of World Broadcasts, September 20, 1980.

Martin Regg Cohn, "In the Forgotten Killing fields," *Toronto Star*, January 26, 2003.

Amy Beth Graves, "Survivors Mark Kent State Shootings," Associated Press, May 4, 2000.

Edward S. Herman, "Pol Pot's Death in the Propaganda System," *Z Magazine*, June 1998.

Boreth Ly, "Devastated Vision(s): The Khmer Rouge Scopic Regime in Cambodia," *Art Journal,* Spring 2003.

McLean's, "A Gloomy Forecast for a Broken Nation," June 3, 1985.

John Pilger, "How Thatcher Gave Pol Pot a Hand," *New Statesman,* April 17, 2000.

James Pringle, "Surviving in the Land That Justice Forgot," *Sunday Tribune* (Ireland), February 16, 2003.

Public Broadcasting System, "The People's Verdict," transcript of *PBS Online News Hour:* "Justice for Pol Pot?" August 6, 1997.

Alan Sipress, "Restoring Pol Pot's Hideout," *Gazette* (Montreal), April 25, 2004.

Videos

Central Independent Television, *Cambodia: The Betrayal: A Special Report by John Pilger,* New York: Filmmakers Library, 1993.

Home Vision Entertainment, *The Red Masters.* Vol. 3: *Pol Pot: Man of Genocide,* 2002.

INA and ARTE France, *S21, the Khmer Rouge Killing Machine.* Brooklyn, NY: First Run/Icarus Films, 2002.

Internet Sources

Cable News Network, "Pol Pot's Relatives Recall Dictator's Childhood," *CNN World News,* August 18, 1997. www.cnn.com/WORLD/9708/18/cambodia/index.html.

David Chandler, "Time 100: Pol Pot," *Time Asia,* August 23–30, 1999. www.time.com/time/asia/asia/magazine/1999/990823/pol_potl.html.

INDEX

Angkar
    meeting of, 60–61
    members of, 60, 62
    policies of, 61
    Pol Pot's paranoia and, 68–69
    spies for, 74
Atkins, Chester, 86

Berlin Youth Festival, 30
bombing raids, U.S., 52
    see also United States, bombing of Cambodia
        by
Buddhism, 28–29

Cambodia
    agreement with France on independence of,
        25–26
    brief independence of, 16
    conflict of, with Vietnam
        evacuations and massacres during, 74
        hardships for country during, 73–74
        Pol Pot's optimism on, 74–75, 79
    constitution of, 34
    expatriates returning to, 76–77
    under French rule, 11–12
    Khmer Empire in, 10–11
    Khmer Rouge prisons and burial sites in, 91
    nationalism in, 14–16
    political parties in, 16–17
    postrevolutionary tensions between Vietnam
        and, 71–72
    prerevolutionary, 11
    at time of Communist takeover, 56
    Vietnamese takeover of, 79–80
    Vietnamese withdrawal from, 87
Cambodian Communists
    crackdown on, 42–43
    goal of, to overthrow Sihanouk, 41–42
    1960 meeting of, 40–41
    recruitment of, 40

see also Khmer Rouge
Chandler, David P., 18, 22, 25, 35, 39, 48, 54, 78,
    79
Chau Seng, 20
Chea Samy, 12
China
    Communist revolution in, 26
    Cultural Revolution in, 47–48
    military aid by, 73
    relations of, with Soviets, 47
    support of, for Pol Pot's exiled regime, 81, 85
    trade embargo of, against Cambodia, 86
    see also Mao Tse-tung
Choeung Ek (Cambodia), 68
Cité Universitaire de Paris, 21–22
civilians
    executions of, 58
    hardships on, caused by Vietnam conflict,
        73–74
    impact of Pol Pot's regime on, 93–94
    mines and, 86
    under People's Republic of Kampuchea rule, 83
    superficial improvements for, 75–76
Collège Norodom Sihanouk (high school), 13–14
communism
    in France, 20, 22, 26, 30–31
    Khmer Student Association's interest in, 26
    Pol Pot's commitment to, 25
    see also Cambodian communists; Khmer
        Student Association; Vietnamese
        Communists
Communist Party of Kampuchea (CPK), 6
    alliance of, with Sihanouk, 53
    Angkar and, 60–62
    change of name to, 49
    constitution under, 63–64
    defeated by Vietnamese, 79
    defections from, 88–90, 92
    in early days of civil war, 54
    during exile, 85

foreign aid and support to, 85–86
overtaking Phnom Penh, 55
post-Vietnamese coalition and, 88
purges within, 68–70, 76
rebellion planned by, 49–50
recruitment into, 50–52
see also Cambodian Communists; Khmer
   Rouge

deaths
   during evacuation of Phnom Penh, 58, 59
   in the Killing Fields, 67–68
   in massacre of Cambodian soldiers, 74
   number of, under Pol Pot, 6, 74, 80
   Pol Pot denying affiliation with, 85
   from U.S. bombings, 51
Democratic Kampuchea (DK), 6
   announcement of, 59
   purges within, 69–70, 76
   see also Communist Party of Kampuchea
Democratic Party
   coup d'état and, 30
   elections of 1955 and, 36, 37
   power of, 16
   violence against, 38

École Technique (school), 19
Etcheson, Craig, 28, 30, 59, 69, 79
Etcheson, David, 94

First Indochina War, 35–36
France
   aid from, to exiled Pol Pot regime, 85
   Cambodia under rule of, 11–12
   German invasion of, 15
   Paris, during 1940s and 1950s, 25
   peace accord of, with Vietnam, 35–36
   signs agreement with Cambodia, 25–26
   study in, 19, 20–27
   Vietnamese Communists and, 27–28
French Communist Party (FCP), 20, 22, 30–31

Gaulle, Charles de, 16
Geneva Conference (1945), 36
Germany, 15

Great Britain, 85, 86
guerrilla resistance groups. *See* Vietminh

Hercombe, Peter, 61
Herman, Edward S., 56
Hiroshima (Japan), bombing of, 16
Ho Chi Minh, 28
Hou Yuon
   Khmer Student Association and, 25
   meeting with Sihanouk and, 54
   in Sangkum Party, 40
   on U.S. imperialism, 36
Hu Nim
   Angkar and, 62
   meeting with Sihanouk and, 54
   Pol Pot's college years and, 14
   in Sangkum Party, 40
   split in Khmer Student Association and, 36
   on U.S. imperialism, 36
Hun Sen, 88

Ieng Sary, 49
   in Angkar, 60, 62
   Berlin Youth Festival and, 30
   at Cambodian Communist Party meeting, 40
   fiancée of, 23–24
   Khmer Student Association and, 24–25
   in Paris, 22
   Pol Pot meets, 19
   sentenced to death, 84–85
   Sihanouk and, 54
   trial of, 83–84
   turns himself in, 88–89
   working as a teacher, 36
Ieng Thirith, 23–24, 62, 89
Indochina, 15
Indochinese Communist Party (ICP), 20, 28, 33
   elections of 1955 and, 36–37

Japan
   presence of, in Cambodia, 15
   World War II and, 16

Kang Kech Leu, 67
Kang Khek, 62

Keng Vannsak, 23
    Khmer Student Association and, 24–25
    Pol Pot's work with, 37, 38
    violence against Democrats and, 38
Keo Meas, 49
Khieu Ponnary. See Saloth Ponnary
Khieu Samphan, 14
    amnesty offered to, 89
    in Angkar, 62
    imprisonment of, 42–43
    Khmer Student Association and, 25
    meeting with Sihanouk and, 54
    new government announced by, 59
    newspaper set up by, 40
    as prime minister, 85
    on U.S. imperialism, 36
Khieu Thirith. See Ieng Thirith
Khmer Communist Party Congress, 40
Khmer people, 10
Khmer People's Party (KPP), 28, 30, 36
Khmer People's Revolutionary Party (KPRP), 28
Khmer Rouge, 45
Khmer Student Association (KSA)
    Berlin Youth Festival and, 30
    cliques within, 24–25
    French Communist Party and, 30–31
    interest of, in communism, 26
    opposition of, to Sihanouk, 25–26
    Pol Pot at meetings of, 26–27
    split on ideologies within, 36
    Vietnamese influence on, 27–28
Khrushchev, Nikita, 47
Khvan Siphan, 14
Kiernan, Ben, 10, 11, 27, 63

Laotian People's Party (LPP), 28
Le Duan, 46
Liberal Party, 37
Lon Nol, 14
    coup d'état by, 52
    disappearance of Tou Sammouth and, 43
    as prime minister, 49
    reaction to riots by, 50
    response to student protests by, 44
Lon Non, 14

Loth Suong (brother), 12
    Pol Pot's contact with, in Paris, 22
    Pol Pot's secrecy with, 32
    realizes his brother is Pol Pot, 78
Luk Khun Meak, 12–13
Ly, Boreth, 69
Lycée Sisowath (school), 13

Mao Tse-tung
    advice from, to Pol Pot, 64
    Pol Pot's meeting with, 47–48
Martin, Marie Alexandrine, 23, 34
Mea Son, 87
media, 77
Mey Mann
    Khmer Student Association and, 25
    on Pol Pot, 20–21, 26
Mey Phat, 20
Monivong, (king), 12
Montparnasse (France), 23

Nagasaki (Japan), bombing of, 16
National Assembly, 16–17, 25
Nixon, Richard, 51
Norodom Ranariddh (prince), 88
Norodom Sihanouk (prince)
    alliance of, with Communist Party of
        Kampuchea, 53
    amnesty offered by, 89
    Communist Party's goal of overthrowing,
        41–42
    constitution revised under, 34
    coup d'état by, 30
    crackdown on Cambodian Communists by,
        42–43
    Khmer Empire and, 11
    martial law under, 32
    meets with Pol Pot, 54
    National Assembly elections and, 17
    opposition to, 25–26
    peasant uprising and, 50
    in postrevolutionary government, 59, 64
    as a private citizen, 38
    removed from power, 52–53
    on Vietnam War, 42, 48–49

after Vietnamese withdrawal, 88

North Korea, 72
Nuon Chea
    amnesty offered to, 89
    in Angkar, 60, 62
    low profile of, 78
    as prime minister, 89
    in Workers Party of Kampuchea, 41

Office 100 (Vietnamese base), 45–46
operations. *See* bombing raids, U.S.

Pach Chhoeun, 16
peasant riots, 50
Pen Saloth (father), 9
People's Republic of Kampuchea (PRK), 80
    changes under, 83
    discovers Pol Pot regime horrors, 82–83
    lack of aid to, 86
    trade embargo against, 86
    trial against Pol Pot regime by, 83–84
Phnom Penh (Cambodia), 12
    Khmer Rouge takeover and, 55, 56
    during Pol Pot's youth, 18
    post-revolution evacuation of, 57–58, 59
Pol Pot
    becomes well known, 77–78
    birth of, 9
    communism and, 26–27
    criticized by Vietnamese, 46–47
    death of, 93
        reactions to, 92
    disappearance of Tou Sammouth and, 43
    double life of, 40
    education of
        early, 9
        high school, 13–14
        in Paris, 19, 20–27
        in Phnom Penh, 12–13
        technical school, 19
    efforts to capture, 92–93
    enemies of, 65–66
    in exile, 81, 86–88
    family background of, 9–10

French Communist Party and, 30–31
    goal of, for Cambodian independence, 8, 18
    health of, 89
    in hiding, 44
    indoctrination of soldiers by, 56–57
    innocence claimed by, 85, 90, 92
    leadership of
        culture of fear during, 74
        effort to replicate Mao plan and, 64–65
        evacuations under, 57–58, 59
        executions under, 58
        secrecy in, 59–60
        superficial changes during, 75–76
    legacy of, 93–94
    low profile of, 78
    meets with Sihanouk, 54
    paranoia of, 68–70, 74
    reaction to defections, 89–90
    secrecy of identity of, 6–7
    sentenced to death, 84–85
    speech on Cambodia's Communist affiliations
        by, 71–72
    teaching by, 39, 40
    trial of, 83–84, 90
    unanswered questions about, 7–8
    Vietnamese and, 29–30
    at Vietnamese base, 45–46
Pracheachon Group, 37

Ratankiri (Cambodia), 49
Rath Sameourn, 22, 36
Ratner, Steven, 90
refugees, 81
riots, 44, 50

Saloth Ponnary (wife), 54
    in Angkar, 62
    after Khmer Rouge defections, 89
    mental illness of, 86–87
    in Paris, 24
    romantic relationship of, with Pol Pot, 38
Saloth Sar. *See* Pol Pot
Sangkum National Assembly, 39
Sangkum Reastr Niyum, 38, 39
Santebal (police force), 66

Second Indochina War, 48
Singapore, 85
Sok Nem (mother), 99
Son Ngoc Thanh, 16
Son Sen, 36, 49, 54
    amnesty offered to, 89
    in Angkar, 62
    execution of, 89–90
    in Sangkum Party, 40
Soviet Union, 47
SS *Jamaique*, 20–21, 31
starvation, 65
student protests, 43–44
S-21 prison, 66–68, 69, 72, 76
Sweden, 85

Ta Mok
    in Angkar, 62
    efforts to capture, 92–93
taxes, export, 50
Thailand, 81–82
Thanhist Democrats, 37
Thayer, Nate, 90
Theravadic Buddhism, 28–29
Thiounn, Mumm, 22–23
    Berlin Youth Festival and, 30
    Khmer Student Association and, 24–25
    Pol Pot's work with, 37
    violence against Democrats and, 38
Tou Sammouth, 40
    disappearance of, 43
    in Workers Party of Kampuchea, 41
Tuol Svang Genocide Museum, 94
Tuol Svay. *See* S-21 prison

Uch Ven, 20
United Front, 53
United States
    bombing of Cambodia by, 50–51
    end of Vietnam War and, 55
    Khmer Student Association's opposition to, 36
    support and aid to Pol Pot's regime by, 81, 85, 86
    trade embargo against Cambodia by, 86

Vietnamese/Cambodian opposition to, 27
UN Security Council, 88

Vann Nath, 66
Vietminh, 18
    Pol Pot joins forces of, 32–35
    Pol Pot stays at base of, 45–46
Vietnamese
    Angkar policy on, 61
    Cambodian attacks and massacres on, 72
    France's peace agreement with, 35–36
    Pol Pot criticized by, 46–47
    Pol Pot on, 28–29, 65–66
    postrevolutionary tensions between Cambodia and, 71–72
    retaliatory raid into Cambodia by, 73
    takeover by, 79–80
    withdrawal from Cambodia by, 87
    see also Cambodia, conflict with Vietnam
Vietnamese Communists
    Cambodian Communists' support for, 40, 41
    influence of, on Khmer Student Association, 27–28
    rice crop taxes and, 50
Vietnamese Workers Party (VWP), 28
Vietnam War (1954–1975), 35–36
    end of, 55
    Sihanouk and, 42, 48–49
violence
    against Democrats, 38
    peasant uprising and, 50
    see also deaths

West Germany, 85
Workers Party of Kampuchea (WPK), 41, 46–47
    see also Cambodian Communists
World Food Program, 86
World War II, 15–16

Youk Chang, 94
Yugoslavia, 22
Yugoslavian television interview, 77
Yun Yat, 62

Picture Credits

About the
Author

Andy Koopmans is the author of a dozen nonfiction books and is also a fiction writer, essayist, and poet. He lives in Seattle, Washington, with his wife Angela Mihm and their pets Bubz, Licorice, and Zachary.

He wishes to thank his editor, Jennifer Skancke, for her continued assistance and excellence, as well as authors David Chandler and Ben Kiernan, whose extensive work serves as the foundation for so much scholarship on Cambodia, including this book. He also wishes to thank Bert Koopmans and John Hawley for making it possible for him to visit Cambodia in 2003.